Sarah Norris is one of the most accomplished and experienced maternity nurses in the UK. She is an expert in her field, and has cared for hundreds of babies during her 25-year career. She has worked with celebrity couples including Sienna Miller and Tom Sturridge, Jessica and James Purefoy, and a number of the Guinness family. Getting her message out to as many families as possible is Sarah's passion and life's work.

This book is dedicated to my parents,
Cynthia and Stanley Norris

I inherited my love of babies from my mother, my love
of words from my father and creativity from them both,
but beyond that I have gained and learned so much more
from them including patience, common sense,
professionalism, duty and the need and ability to express
myself and communicate with others. Not forgetting the
rather 'unique' Norris sense of humour, which has helped
keep me sane (ish!) through the years.

I have never received anything less from them
than unconditional love, support and encouragement
all of which have given me the strength and courage
to follow my literary dream.

I am proud to be your daughter.

xxx

The
Baby Detective

*Solve your baby problems
your way*

SARAH NORRIS

First published in 2017
by Orion Spring,
an imprint of The Orion Publishing Group Ltd
Carmelite House, 50 Victoria Embankment
London EC4Y 0DZ

An Hachette UK Company

1 3 5 7 9 10 8 6 4 2

With thanks to Andrew Collier Photography for all internal images.

Every effort has been made to ensure that the information in the
book is accurate. The information in this book may not be applicable
in each individual case so it is advised that professional medical
advice is obtained for specific health matters and before changing
any medication or dosage. Neither the publisher nor author accepts any
legal responsibility for any personal injury or other damage or loss
arising from the use of the information in this book. In addition if you
are concerned about your diet or exercise regime and wish to change
them, you should consult a health practitioner first.

A CIP catalogue record for this book
is available from the British Library.

Hardback ISBN: 978 1 4091 6841 6
Trade Paperback ISBN: 978 1 4091 6842 3

Printed in Great Britain by CPI Group (UK) Ltd, Croydon, CR0 4YY

www.orionbooks.co.uk

ORION
SPRING

Contents

Contents

Contents

Contents

Introduction

This book differs from many other baby care books in that it does not suggest you can be a perfect parent, dictate which parenting style is best or tell you the 'right way' to care for your baby.

Instead, the approach will be to guide you through an investigative process that will help you identify *when* something is going wrong, *what* the problem is, *why* it is happening, and will provide you with the information you need in order to devise and implement realistic solutions that suit you, your baby and your whole family.

You will learn how to **AIM**: that is, Assess, Investigate and Modify your baby's and your own behaviour. All you need in order to do this is to keep an open mind, have faith in yourself and trust the process that is developed in the following pages.

At the end, you will be a confident, competent parent capable of recognising and meeting your baby's needs and adjusting every aspect of baby care to solve current and future problems and meet every new challenge. This confidence will allow you to relax and enjoy your journey with your baby instead of wasting time being worried and stressed.

You will not need to rely on books or experts, because *you* will be the expert on your own baby – you will write your own book.

Who am I?
What do I do and why?

As I am asking you to trust me, I had better introduce myself and explain why my experiences in baby care will provide a firm basis for the diagnostic approach developed throughout this book.

I am a maternity nurse, and my job is to attend clients when they have a new baby. I stay in the home working twenty-four hours a day, six days a week for a few days or weeks, or sometimes a few months.

The purpose of a maternity nurse is to help the mother get over the birth, help the family adjust to the new baby and leave them fully prepared to take over when we leave. To do this, we advise and encourage parents as they take care of baby, covering such things as feeding, changing, bathing, sleeping, winding, routines and development. We are responsible for bottle-sterilising and feed preparation, baby's laundry and helping with other equipment.

We also act as troubleshooters, to try to help when there is a problem or an emergency.

I have been a maternity nurse for twenty-five years now; a quarter of a century's worth of sleepless nights, endless feeds and too many nappy changes to even think about.

That's twenty-five years of observing babies, siblings, pets and parents, solving problems, devising and adjusting sleeping and feeding routines and listening to, and dealing with, the fears and confusion of the parents.

I have cared for hundreds of families: with twins, triplets, premature babies, reflux babies; families that have experienced a cot death; families that have struggled with fertility. I have resuscitated a baby that stopped breathing.

I am not someone who walks in, hands out advice and walks away again.

In caring for these babies, I am there every minute of every working day. If I give bad advice, I have to deal with the consequences of it.

I get involved with the families (for better or worse), sharing the sleeplessness, the stress, the joys and the laughter. I have held a baby as he fought to come back to life, and have held a sobbing mother who was told her baby would not live.

I am not trying to blow my own trumpet, but to convince you that I am speaking not just from a position of experience, but from a position of compassion.

I love the babies, every last one of them, and care deeply about their parents. I resent very much the pressure, stress and confusion that seem to have become associated with modern-day parenting, and which is preventing people from being able to relax and enjoy their precious time with their new baby.

One of my main aims with clients is to alleviate this pressure and stress, and that is what I am intending to do with this book.

During my time as a maternity nurse, I have seen every aspect of baby care carried out in every possible way by people with different personalities, lifestyles and ages, from different social classes, income brackets and cultures. I have come to the conclusion that, though there are a few ways of getting it wrong, there are many more ways of getting it right.

There are plenty of books and experts who will tell you that they have 'the answer', the holy grail of parenting, the one way that will work, the one routine you should follow or the parenting method that will solve all your problems.

Like the gambler who thinks he has a foolproof system to beat the casinos, they are deceiving both themselves and you.

You are unique; your family is unique and your baby is unique, which means your parenting will also be unique. These external 'expert' voices often do not recognise or value this uniqueness.

There is no 'best way' – just the most appropriate approach for you and your baby, for that particular moment or situation, or sometimes simply a practical coping mechanism for that exhausted moment after no sleep, a baby with colic and visitors who have stayed too long.

There is also, most definitely, no 'perfect parenting'. This is an image often created by us, born of a totally understandable desire to be good parents.

The redeeming truth is that this idea of unattainable perfection is also totally unnecessary: nothing and no one around you is perfect, so let it go, along with all the negative emotions that go with it such as guilt, stress, worry, confusion, despair, anger, self-recrimination and regret.

The wonderful fact is that, for the first four weeks, babies want only four things from you. They want:

- a full tummy
- lots of cuddles
- lots of sleep
- freedom from discomfort and pain

. . . and that's it.

After three or four weeks, you can start adding more stimulation and interaction into the mix.

This is the basic recipe for the first three months.

What's even more wonderful is that babies don't really mind

who is providing all these things, which takes the pressure off mums and means that dads, partners, relatives, friends, nurses, can all help provide what baby needs, and you can accept this help without any fear of damaging the bonding process in any way whatsoever.

Over the years I've helped hundreds of families doing a job that I love, but recently I've begun to experience frustration at the plight of many families who lack confidence in their baby care capabilities. They seem to be struggling to cope with dubious advice, lack of positive support, contradictory approaches, universal solutions that claim to fit all babies and promise perfection and, most perplexing of all, the professional, media and social media criticism, judgement and intimidation that is all too rife.

When I started writing this book, it forced me to analyse just what it is that I do, and why, when I leave a job, the parents are confident and well prepared to take over and continue on their own.

I have always known that I am not a 'baby whisperer' – I do not possess any magical baby-taming powers. Everything I do you can learn too, with time and patience and an open mind.

What I am, first and foremost, is a teacher. I love sharing what I have experienced. This inner teacher is urging me to write this book, and I have found the investigative approach crucial in identifying the unique nature of individual parenting problems.

Second, but equally important, I am an investigator.

In employing an investigative approach, I focus on the parents as the starting point. Many questions have to be asked, and the answers require me to remain objective in order to identify possible problematic attitudes and expectations the parents may have regarding their baby.

Interpretations of the parents' body language and behaviour can clarify some of their feelings towards the baby, each other and the situation. This process needs to be sensitively handled, and must take note of the difficulties some people have in revealing their inner thoughts and emotions to a stranger in the household.

I need to be able to notice when someone is anxious, stressed, afraid, annoyed, exhausted, withdrawn, obsessive, uncertain, depressed, or exhibiting behavioural patterns which might impair the establishing of a positive relationship between parent and child.

I need to be able to notice how the different people within the home, and those visiting it, affect and interact with each other.

I need to see how they communicate, or struggle to communicate, with me and with each other, and what obstacles might be getting in the way of this such as fear, ego, guilt, insecurity, over-confidence or lack of confidence.

I need to use all this to find the best way to talk to the parents and the immediate family, to build trust and to be able to move forward through appropriate and personalised advice developed from my extensive experience. The assimilation of this advice should speed up the progress towards capable parenting and allow the parents to relax and enjoy the experience.

What is AIM?

Going back to the acronym **AIM**: you need to be able to accurately **Assess** what is going on. I stress accurately because sometimes it is hard to see past personal emotions, or the perceptions of those closest to us – we assume, we make excuses or we blame.

An example of this might be the mum being angry with the dad because he doesn't offer to help change nappies, but the reality might be that the first few times he did offer to help, the overcorrective attitude of the mum was off-putting rather than encouraging.

By being observant, open-minded and honest, you will be much better able to see what is really happening at any particular moment. This will allow you to read your baby's body language and get to know their character, so you can easily interpret what they are trying to tell you.

Once you can see what is happening in any given situation, you can **Investigate** using your skills to question yourself and each other in order to identify and solve problems. Guidance will be offered in Chapter 2 to ascertain what factors might be affecting your baby's behaviour and moods, for example hunger, tiredness, overstimulation, pain, boredom, illness, over-handling or discomfort.

When this is coupled with what you have learnt about your baby's character, it will allow you to move on to the next step: to **Modify** your baby's environment, and your own actions, to solve whatever problem is occurring.

What's more, you will learn to apply this approach as a mental process that you can use to predict what might happen in future situations, to help you plan for new stages in your baby's development or to cope with disruptions such as illness, travel, trips out and occasions such as weddings or christenings, and that will allow you to adapt routines accordingly.

Most parents figure all this out for themselves by the time they are on their second or third child, but that's no consolation for those on their first or second baby. That's why I have written this book: to speed the process up.

I would like you, as far as possible with the lack of sleep, the endless nappy changes and baby's uncanny knack of waking up just when your supper is ready, to enjoy every single moment with your first baby – to be able to relax, knowing that you have everything under control.

I would like you to feel that you have the necessary skills to cope with whatever behaviour is expressed, and that you will be able to rise to any challenge that fate – or everyday life – may send your way.

Finally, I would like you to have the confidence and faith in yourself as a parent to know that the parenting choices *you* make are the right ones for **you, your baby and your family as a whole**, and that you do not need the opinions or approval of family, friends, social media, other mums and our ever-critical society.

Looking at parenthood in forensic analysis terms may seem like an unusual approach, but in reality, that is what you would be doing on a daily basis without even realising it.

To give you a better idea of what I mean, the next chapter will be an in-depth description of a troubleshooting job I went to a few years ago, and I will guide you, step by step, through what I saw, what I asked, what I observed and how the parents and I 'solved the case' and sorted the problem.

Throughout the rest of the chapters, using case studies we will cover the most common problems usually encountered during the first six months, including the process of winding baby, which will be dealt with in great detail and with clear illustrations. I will also cover questions regarding feeding, sleeping, crying, swaddling, routines, development, play, travel, illness, weaning and what 'normal' appearance and behaviour are for new babies.

I will share with you many tried and tested hints, tips, strategies and money-saving ideas that will help make your parenting journey easier. At the end of the book, you will be an expert on your own baby. Not anyone else's; yours.

1.

How to be your own Baby Detective

AN EXAMPLE OF A BABY DETECTIVE INVESTIGATION

To begin with, I will share with you the procedure I follow when I arrive at the home of new clients, particularly if I am in the role of troubleshooter, where there is a specific problem.

I will explain exactly what I am doing to enable you to reproduce the same process yourselves when dealing with your own baby.

This procedure is not just for solving big problems, when things have gone seriously wrong; it is also for day-to-day fixing and tweaking and sorting out minor problems to prevent them from escalating into major disasters, and for thinking about and planning changes to your daily routine.

CASE STUDY

Two-week windy-baby troubleshooting job in London

BRIEF First baby, six weeks old. This breastfed baby apparently has colic, cries all the time and can't be put down in his moses basket, needs holding to sleep. Dad works fairly long hours; mum is at home on maternity leave. Both parents are exhausted and desperate for help.

ENVIRONMENT After meeting the parents and noticing that they were practically grey with exhaustion, a quick glance around told me two things: first, that the normal state of the house seemed to be neat and tidy, with everything put away, but that baby stuff was randomly heaped around in piles, with little sense of organisation. This might not seem relevant, but it was an indication of an abnormal sense of chaos that would not help the parents' mood in general.

Second, it struck me that mum appeared to live on the sofa full-time. There were TV remotes, pillows, blankets, magazines, snacks, drinks, phone and iPad with chargers, breast pads, tablets, even a spare T-shirt. While this was practical, it suggested a siege situation, with mum trapped in one place, which was not great for her mental and emotional well-being.

As I went to wash my hands, I noticed that the pram was almost invisible under a pile of post, laundry and other stuff and didn't look very accessible, which was also unusual as prams are usually in pretty regular use.

I asked both parents what their days were like and they replied with the following:

Mum did indeed spend her whole life on the sofa, almost from the moment she got up to the moment she went to bed. She had everything she needed on hand because she didn't have the energy to go looking for things, and because once baby was asleep on her she didn't dare move in case he woke up and cried again (*trapped*).

Baby screamed in the pram so they didn't go for walks or get out to any baby groups or meet other mums (*isolated*).

Baby was so difficult and mum so tired that she rarely asked anyone round to visit; it was easier just to manage on her own (*lonely*).

She had daytime TV on all day for company (*bored*).

She ate snack food throughout the day, then they had a ready meal or takeaway in the evening so they could eat quickly in shifts while one of them held the baby (*poor nutrition*).

The day was bad enough, but they dreaded the nights even more (*sleep deprivation*).

Dad had to work, so he slept in the spare room during the week, leaving mum to deal with baby on her own (*possible cause of resentment*).

They were both stressed and exhausted and not enjoying their baby.

LIFE BEFORE BABY At this point it was important for me to ask what their normal, pre-baby life was like so that I could get a sense of how far off balance they were, and what it would take to get things more normal and comfortable for them. Questions were asked tactfully, and the replies listened to carefully without assumption or judgement.

They confirmed that they liked the house tidy and organised and loved to cook healthy food. They also loved to go out for walks, and enjoyed socialising both at home and out and about.

Mum, on her maternity leave, had enjoyed being active, hardly ever watched TV, but now baby had arrived desperately wanted to go out and do what other mums were doing, but felt like there was no dynamic to the day, just the same relentless feed, hold, feed, hold . . . a black pit of parenting.

As the parents were talking I watched their expressions and body language, and was heartened to see that though they were stressed, there was no anger towards the baby, and, more amazingly, no tension between each other. The situation had them working, as best they could, as a team, and the mum genuinely had no problem with the dad sleeping in the spare room. This was important because it would make finding and applying solutions so much easier if their own couple dynamic was sound.

It is important to note that during the discussion, I am listening without judgement, assumption or criticism, which you will find harder than you think when you try this for yourselves.

TYPICAL DAY I then asked them to talk me through a typical day, and listened and watched carefully to note any discrepancies between what they thought and said they were doing and what was actually happening. (Not because they were deliberately lying, but because they were inexperienced parents and in a fog of exhaustion and confusion and it would be easier for an objective and experienced outsider to see things a little more clearly.)

They indicated that baby fed well to start with, but got progressively worse as the feed went on and even worse as the day progressed. He wouldn't settle down to play or sleep and was crying, wriggling or restless. If they got him to sleep in their arms and then tried to put him down in his moses basket, he woke up and screamed, and they had to start rocking, cuddling and soothing all over again, so they had pretty much stopped trying and just sat and held him so that he got some sleep.

This went on all day, and baby had major meltdown screaming sessions in the evening until they fed him to repletion and he fell into a deep sleep late at night. Then he went down in his moses basket and slept there for about three hours, but subsequently woke for a feed and started fussing and crying again, which meant that mum was up from about 3 a.m. feeding and holding baby and dozing in a chair because she was afraid of falling asleep with him in bed and rolling on him. They did try co-sleeping, but he cried when put down next to them, so they gave that up.

OBSERVATIONS The next step was for me to observe them feed baby, and I was relieved to see that that, at least, was going well. Mum's position was good, as was her technique for getting baby to latch. The latch itself was secure, and baby knew what to do: he got straight onto the breast and, after the initial let-down sucking (short, rapid sucks), he settled down to good, strong, rhythmical drinking and swallowing. There was nothing to fault there at all.

She kept him on the breast for as long as possible, because once he came off it was difficult to get him back on and sometimes that first part of the feed was all baby could manage. They dreaded him coming off after only a few minutes because this indicated the beginning of distress for baby.

WINDING Once he came off, mum winded him briefly by putting him over her shoulder and rubbing his back. He did a small burp, so she went back to trying to feed him, but I noted how wriggly he was and suspected that he had a lot more wind that needed to come out before he could feed again comfortably.

Mum said she thought he was hungry so kept trying to feed, but though he latched on quite hungrily, he came off again very quickly, which is another indication of wind trapped inside his stomach.

When I suggested we try to wind him more thoroughly, they both told me that the midwife at the hospital had informed them that breastfed babies didn't require winding, so they didn't need to bother too much.

Myth: breastfed babies do not need winding.

Truth: all babies get wind, regardless of how they are fed.

This explained a great deal, and indicated a likely source of the problem. I had to explain that breastfed babies can get just as much wind as bottle-fed babies, even if they have a perfect latch.

This is a common misconception which I encounter all the time – the people who perpetuate it are doing a lot of damage.

It is always better to ignore the *method* of feeding, and focus on your own individual baby and learn exactly how much wind is normal for him, regardless of how he is fed and any related expectations, as in this case.

Once I had explained this and demonstrated how much more wind I could get from the baby when I persisted, they both became upset at the fact that they had, unknowingly, left their baby in pain for six weeks. They felt terribly guilty and very distressed.

I was able to reassure them by pointing out that this was actually a good result because it was very easily fixed and meant that baby probably didn't have colic. I promised them they would learn how to be really effective winders and that we would be able to sort the problem.

The next feed was supervised closely, and when baby came off the breast I showed them how to wind him by trying lots of different positions, using lots of slow-motion movements, lying him down and picking him up, and also how to gently 'jiggle' the baby's tummy or midriff to be able to hear when there was a bubble inside.

> The trick to effective winding is to use lots of different positions and techniques, so if something is not working after thirty seconds, stop and try something else.

I kept going until no more wind could be felt or heard. Then we tried baby back at the breast, and he fed much more calmly for longer than usual. Every time he came off he was winded thoroughly, and we used nappy changes to wake him up and to dislodge any more bubbles. We repeated this until he seemed calm and well fed and then I started to talk to them about sleep, while baby rested face down over my knees for further winding.

SWADDLING I suggested swaddling him to help him sleep and to be more likely to cope with the transfer from my arms to his moses basket, but mum said very quickly that he hated being swaddled; he didn't like his arms being restricted and always screamed.

This was surprising, because I had never come across any baby that didn't like being swaddled if it was done properly.

I suggested that it was perhaps more likely that it was the parents who didn't like the thought of their arms being restricted, and that they were projecting their own feelings onto their baby. This is a very common occurrence and happens over many different aspects from feeding, to routine, sleep, dressing, bathing and more.

The truth is that new babies are very different from adults, and are totally happy with lots of things their parents might not like the idea of.

You have to take into account, too, that they are not carbon copies of their parents, but have their own unique personalities and character traits which require handling in particular ways.

I described the swaddle as being like a big, portable hug, which means the baby feels comforted and held even when he has been put down, making it much easier to transfer baby from the parent's arms to the moses basket.

I also explained that one of the reasons he may have screamed was because they had tried to swaddle him while he still had wind in his tummy; in effect, they were trapping him in the swaddle with the tummy pain, which would be enough to make anyone cry.

I asked them to trust me, to let me try swaddling and see what happened, and that if he really hated it we could always take it off again.

They agreed, and the sleepy baby was wrapped firmly in my preferred swaddle, the Miracle Blanket. I was very gentle and my movements smooth and baby barely stirred . . . no screaming.

He was cuddled upright for a couple of minutes in case any more wind needed to come up (swaddling can often help release more wind), then very slowly put down in his moses basket. This had been lined with a little sheepskin fleece to make it comfortable, and then a cotton cell cot blanket had been rolled lengthwise to make a long sausage shape and placed around his body from the shoulders down around his feet and back up again on the other side so he was in a cosy little nest. Then I tucked him in with another little blanket . . . and he slept!

Neither parent could believe their eyes. They stood there, rooted to the spot, just looking at their baby sleeping peacefully in his moses basket for the first time in his six weeks of life.

They had a normal, non-colicky baby who needed them to help him burp and sleep, and the worst was now over.

Mum promptly burst into tears of relief and we sat down and had tea and cake while they calmed down and started to process everything that had happened.

> Remember, as a new parent you will make mistakes — lots of them — but babies are very forgiving. They live in the 'now', which means that they don't stress over the past or worry about the future, so once you have sorted whatever is wrong with them they are completely happy and you have nothing to feel guilty about.

MOVING FORWARD I explained that baby was as exhausted as they were and that, if we continued to make it easy for him to burp and sleep, he would probably sleep for the next couple of days while he caught up. I suggested they do the same, and leave the winding and settling to me so that I could get to know him and what sort of winding techniques would work best for him. This would mean I would be in a much better position to pass all this information on to the parents, and it would give them the break they so desperately needed, and this is what we did.

Mum still fed baby, but I supervised and winded and settled him to sleep and dealt with him if he woke up, which he rarely did.

I explained that this sleepy few days were mimicking the normal sleepy first two weeks of baby's life, giving everyone a chance to adapt and settle in, and that once he was recovered he would be absolutely fine: no lasting damage or emotional trauma or damage to bonding. Then we would have the fun of finding out who he really was, as he would be relaxed enough for his own personality to show through.

For the first two weeks of life a baby is still exhausted from the birth, so they often sleep a great deal, leading parents to believe they have an angel baby or to worry in case something is wrong. This is totally normal, so just enjoy it and use the relative calm to rest after the birth. After two weeks, baby starts waking up more, showing their true temperament and needing more active management, so be prepared for the change.

I was booked for two weeks, and by working with the parents and following the investigative process, we had 'solved the crime' in six hours.

They were eager students, and very quickly learnt how to reproduce my winding techniques and results. They learnt how to look honestly at their lives and personalities and devise the best routine that suited them and their baby, rather than trying to use something they had read in a book or an idealised version of perfect parenting that was unattainable and impractical.

I also showed them how to work flexibility into this routine, and how to adjust it if things went wrong and how to think clearly enough to do their own troubleshooting.

REGAINING CONFIDENCE They had lost confidence in themselves as parents, so we worked on rebuilding that, arming them with lots of hints, tips and strategies that I had discovered over the years that would make life easier for both parents and baby.

We worked through everything that had been too much for them previously, going out for walks with baby in the pram, attending and hosting play dates and going to baby groups. They went shopping and to the doctor's, and out for dinner as a couple and had friends round for supper. Basically we defined what would be a 'normal' life for this particular family and then integrated their baby into that life.

Once things were a lot calmer, they had the chance to discover just who their baby was, what character traits he displayed and how that might affect their baby care provision, and they learnt how to play with him and have fun. The loveliest moment was on the fifth day when he smiled at them for the first time.

Once baby was properly winded, he settled down to being a normal, healthy, happy little boy, and turned out to have a very sunny nature, always ready with a smile – so different from how he had been before.

I stayed in touch with the family for a while in case they needed more help, but they didn't. They had a rough start, but from it they learnt to be confident, practical and effective parents.

SUMMARY Many of the difficult situations new parents find themselves in have a common cause: they are the result of a minor problem going undetected long enough to develop into a major one.

My aim in sharing this investigative approach is to teach you how to recognise the minor problems early on, and to deal with them before they can escalate and cause serious disruption to your family life.

In the next chapter we will discuss the different factors that can affect your baby and relate them back to this case study using my **Assess**, **Investigate**, **Modify** approach. I will give you a strategic framework of questions to ask yourselves that will allow you to prevent or solve any parenting challenges you may encounter.

How you do this for yourselves

The starting point for any effective problem-solving strategy is objectivity. That is, how to look at a situation and see what is really happening, as opposed to what you assume or think or believe is happening, because your perception is being affected by many different factors.

During the pregnancy, parents spend a lot of time wondering what life as a parent will be like, and build dreams and visions of family life, which is natural and wonderful.

The un-wonderful part can come when baby arrives, if the reality doesn't match your dreams.

Maybe the labour didn't go as planned, or breastfeeding was more difficult or painful than you thought, or you didn't realise how tired you would be or how anxious or worried you would find yourself.

> The best thing you can do to avoid shock, disappointment, guilt or regret is to go into the birth with an open mind. Make plans, yes. Have preferences, yes, but be fully prepared for the fact that it is unlikely to go exactly as planned. Remember: all that matters in the end is that mother and baby get through it safely – everything else after that is just window dressing!

The sheer weight of responsibility for this new life can be overwhelming for some people, and either parent may be responding differently to the way you thought you would.

If things go drastically wrong, you may feel like your world and your dreams are crashing down around you, bringing related emotions such as disappointment, guilt, frustration, anger, resentment, fear and uncertainty.

These are all powerful emotions, and they colour your thinking and judgement, making it very hard to see clearly enough to identify problems and find solutions.

You will need to be able to step back, and this is why I have chosen to use the investigative analogy, because it will help you to distance yourself from the emotions that may be clouding the issue.

Becoming your own detective

Everyone has, at some time or another, watched a crime show on TV, and we all know how investigators work. They visit the crime scene, look for clues and question suspects and bystanders. They try to find out what really happened, in what order and why.

Just put yourself in the investigator's shoes. Let go of who you are at that particular moment, of what you are feeling; forget blame and guilt. It seems to be a common storyline in crime shows that one of the investigators gets too emotionally involved in what is happening, their judgement is skewed and they are unable to do their job properly. This is a situation I frequently encounter in my work.

Parents may blame themselves, or each other. They begin to think the baby is misbehaving deliberately. They think they are failing, and are bad parents. They start to feel hopeless and helpless, and confusion sets in as they lose all confidence in themselves. They second-guess every decision they make and ask advice from everyone they can think of, which only adds to the confusion.

> Remember when you feel like this that you are *not* alone! No matter what you are feeling, I promise you that there are other parents out there feeling just as lonely and confused as you are. Keep going and have faith in yourself – you are a great parent!

Have you ever found yourself having an argument with someone, knowing inside that you are being unreasonable but somehow unable to prevent yourself; or made excuses for you or your partner's behaviour instead of confronting it; or overthought something to the point of confusion? If so, then you know how hard it is to stop these behaviour patterns and face the problem squarely. But this is exactly what you will have to learn to do when your baby arrives.

Your baby will need you to find a way to become calm and objective enough to figure out what they need in order to be able to feed and sleep and be happy and healthy.

I would like to stress again that every single person reading this is capable of figuring out what is going wrong with their baby care routine and finding a solution. All you need is to keep an open mind, be completely honest, have faith in yourselves and each other and work through the process.

2.

Clues

WHAT AFFECTS YOUR BABY?

Detectives don't just investigate crimes, they also investigate mysteries, and babies are, without a doubt, the biggest mystery you are ever likely to encounter.

They are such an amazing mixture of confusing and contradictory responses and behaviours that it is a wonder anybody ever manages to understand and manage them at all – but they do, and so will you.

Eventually, through much trial and error and daily exposure to all their nuances and habits, we start to see patterns emerging and discover how baby's environment, their biology and our behaviour all interact and affect baby for better or worse. Once we know this, we can learn to manage them and their environment to create effective baby care strategies, but to reach this point we must first 'solve' our babies, which is no easy matter.

In solving any mystery we need a starting point, and in this case it's twofold. First, we need to be able to identify and interpret clues and, once we can successfully do this, we need to establish a baseline. By this I mean decide what measures need to be in place

24

for your baby to be so calm and comfortable that they can eat efficiently, sleep peacefully and be content when they are awake. Once we know this, we can recognise when things are going wrong and set about trying to fix them.

The problem is, of course, that these requirements can differ from baby to baby, and sometimes from day to day or even minute to minute, so we need to be as fluid and organic in our thinking as babies are in their behaviour.

A vital part of any investigation is to search for clues, but in order to do this, we need to know what those clues might look like, so this chapter will explore what factors might be affecting both you and your baby and how to recognise them.

What affects your baby?

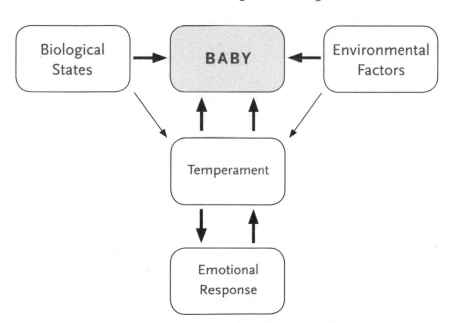

The above diagram is an overview of the different types of factors that affect our baby every second of their lives from the moment they are born.

ENVIRONMENTAL FACTORS These are factors that are external to the baby, that they have no control over but which still directly affect them. They include temperature, light, noise, air movement, physical position, handling and emotional atmosphere.

BIOLOGICAL STATES This refers to everything that comes from the babies themselves, which can only be felt by them, the effects of which we can only guess at. They include hunger, thirst, tiredness, discomfort, pain, illness, insecurity and fear.

TEMPERAMENT This may reveal itself via the baby's thresholds or tolerances for patience, pain, exhaustion, boredom and noise as well as their own personal requirements for security and social interaction or comfort, and sleep.

EMOTIONAL RESPONSE is the way in which the biological and environmental factors impact the baby's personality, creating a reaction which may be positive or negative, and, if negative, can be the trigger for a major meltdown or downward spiral of behaviour.

Environmental factors

I usually start with this because it is the most obvious thing I notice when I encounter a situation for the first time. Because I myself am affected as soon as I walk into the room, it can give me a starting point for investigating.

The environmental factors are ones which surround the baby externally, affecting their senses of sight, hearing, smell and touch (also taste, but that doesn't often cause problems in young babies). These can be obvious things such as light, noise and temperature, but also less obvious ones such as strong smells, their own position, their clothing, their nappy, how they are being held or handled and also the emotional atmosphere in the room.

What is helpful to remember is that these factors can affect babies very differently from the way they affect adults, which is why objectivity and an open mind are very useful when considering them.

Temperature

The temperature of a room may be comfortable for you, but is it comfortable for the baby? What temperature are *you* used to? How many jumpers are *you* wearing? How many layers does baby have on? How many blankets?

You also need to consider the differences in ability to regulate body temperature. Babies have a large surface area with a small body mass, meaning they warm up and cool down a lot more quickly than we do, and they also have less subcutaneous body fat, which normally insulates against heat loss. This means they are a lot less efficient at controlling their own body temperature beyond a very narrow range, so can become uncomfortable in minutes.

I have arrived at a job on a warm day where the adults were wearing shorts and T-shirts so had put their new baby in just a sleeveless vest, but baby was visibly cold. His feet and hands were slightly blue and cold to the touch, extending further up the arms and legs, and he was making unhappy sounds. The parents hadn't realised this meant the baby was cold simply because no one had explained to them the necessity to keep checking, and because they couldn't see any shivering. They were concerned that they had made a serious mistake, but I explained that newborn babies don't yet have the shivering mechanism, and we put baby in a long-sleeved sleep suit, cuddled him for half an hour to warm him up, then he settled happily for the rest of the afternoon in his pram outside with the family – no harm done.

A good tip is always to have baby in one more layer than you have on yourself.

The only real way to gauge accurately if your baby is comfortable temperature-wise is *to get to know your own baby's normal temperature tendencies*: what colour are their hands and feet normally (some can look slightly blue but be perfectly warm everywhere else)? Check them frequently by touching the skin on their hands, feet and head and by putting your hand on their chest and back.

I also touch my lips to the baby's skin as they are so temperature-sensitive. I am constantly doing this, and find it becomes a very precise way to monitor them and prevents you from making assumptions.

A baby who is too cold may appear pale and restless or not able to settle to sleep, or may wake frequently.

A baby who is too hot may appear pink or red in the face, be restless, agitated or very angry and unhappy, often crying and being difficult to calm down, or may gulp milk at feeds due to thirst. They may also sleep deeply, much more than usual, and not wake as usual for their feeds.

New parents are often worried by unexplained rashes, so be aware that it can be common for babies to get a red, raised heat rash when they have been a bit too warm for a while. As long as the rash blanches when pressed and there is no sign of fever or illness, this sort of rash does not need any treatment and gradually fades on its own over a few hours. It can take a few days to go completely and may occasionally reappear whenever baby gets hot, such as when crying or being held for long periods. If you have any doubts then always get baby checked out just to be on the safe side.

Noise

Noise is another environmental factor that can affect babies, but in very different ways. Some babies are happy to have plenty of noise around them, but when tired or overstimulated find it too much for them to deal with. It is quite common when I suggest the baby may be upset due to the noise level for the parents to say, 'Oh, but this is what it is normally like', and I have to explain that at this particular moment, in this particular mood baby has had enough and just needs some peace and quiet.

Other babies are more sensitive and need quiet all the time, which should be respected to a certain degree, but for their own sake I often advise parents to use white noise or a radio or music when baby is sleeping so they don't get used to complete silence.

If you're using a radio, choose a station that is mostly talk, without adverts if possible, so the voices become a steady background without the sudden interruption of loud music.

This might sound counter-intuitive, but we have to be practical, because if baby gets used to sleeping in silence, they will learn *only* to sleep in silence, which means that the parents can never be out of the house at sleep times or have noisy visitors or workmen in the house.

This is one of the downsides of very strict routines that require baby always to sleep in the nursery in silence. The parents are so restricted that serious isolation problems can arise, and may contribute to postnatal depression (PND). It can also cause upset if a second child comes along and the firstborn cannot cope with the noise.

A baby disturbed by noise may refuse to feed or settle to sleep and may wake frequently, appear agitated and cry or scream inconsolably.

The simplest solution is to remove baby to a quiet room and give them time to calm down either by cuddling, pacing, rocking, using a pacifier or distracting them with a nappy change before trying to do anything with them such as feed or settle to sleep.

Many babies enjoy being on their changing mats, so if they are upset try changing baby's nappy as a way of distracting them and giving them a chance to calm down.

Light

Babies are more sensitive to light than older children and adults, so you need to be aware of this but not overcompensate and keep them in gloom and half-light. I have worked with parents who automatically turned off the lights when baby was in the room to the point where I could barely see what I was doing, or they constantly tried to shield baby's eyes, which is mostly unnecessary. As long as the light isn't glaring directly into baby's eyes, they should be OK; baby needs practice at adjusting to different light levels.

One situation where bright light could be a problem is when baby is overtired or overstimulated, when it just adds to whatever is wrong and makes things worse.

The solution is to lower the lights or draw the curtains, take baby indoors if outside or remove baby to a darkened room, giving them the chance to calm down and relax before trying to settle to sleep or feed.

> If you are out and about but feel your baby would benefit from less light, try pulling a thin cotton hat down over their eyes.

Handling

This is much more common a problem than people realise. Babies are such wonderful, cuddle-able little bundles, and everyone is so excited to visit and get to hold them that sometimes baby is passed around from person to person for hours at a time as different friends and relatives come to call. Some of these may be a bit clumsy or not very adept at handling baby, and while some babies don't mind at all, and can put up with it for a while before getting grouchy, others hate it from the beginning. This may be embarrassing or inconvenient but must be respected and their need for peace catered for.

Obviously parents want to be able to show off their new baby as much as possible, but all that is needed is for the timing of handling to be managed with respect to baby's needs. This may mean that visitors only get to meet babies once they are well fed and winded and well rested, rather than just before a feed or nap-time when baby's patience is running low.

It may also help to swaddle your baby quite firmly before they are passed around, as it makes them feel more secure while at the same time being easier for less practised people to hold them.

Once it is clear that baby has had enough, it is the parents' or carers' job to intervene and rescue baby.

Most babies make it quite plain when they have had enough of being passed around and handled by crying and screaming, so the best way to help them is for one person to take them to a quiet room and do something soothing involving *minimal handling* to help them become calm and relaxed.

This might involve walking around, or putting them under a mobile if they are old enough to appreciate it, or lying them on their back on your lap so you can talk to them perhaps with a re-assuring hand placed somewhere on their body (still, not rubbing or patting).

One of my favourite ways to calm them is to rock gently in a rocking chair while holding them to my chest but facing outward so that the movement is soothing, they can be distracted by the room but are not being bothered by too much handling. Sometimes swaddling helps but sometimes it makes things worse, so use trial and error and see what works. Remember, pacifiers are great tools for helping them relax.

We often feel when something is wrong with the baby that we have to 'do something', and the more they cry the more we feel we have to act, unintentionally escalating the problem, when the reality might be that less is more and baby just needs us to back off a little.

It may help protective parents if they are the ones who pass their baby from one person to the next so that they can retain an element of control as to who handles their baby.

OVER-HANDLING AND REFLUX Over-handling can also be a problem with a reflux baby or one that gets a lot of wind as it can take much patting, rubbing, moving, and so on to try to dislodge the wind. This can sometimes get too much for the baby, especially if they are tired, in pain from reflux or hungry and wanting the rest of the feed. They get distressed and upset and it can be very difficult to know exactly why they are crying. Obviously you still need to get the wind up to make baby comfortable, but it is a good idea to give them a break for five to ten minutes to try to soothe and calm them.

Laying baby under a mobile is a good way of helping them relax and recover from over-handling. If baby suffers from reflux, you can put them in their bouncy chair in their cot so they can still enjoy the mobile even if it is from the side.

When feeding a difficult or reflux baby, I myself am sometimes guilty of trying to get a feed over with as soon as I can (especially if I am feeling tired or frustrated). Trying to push ahead when baby is irate can be a false economy of time, making them even more upset, whereas giving baby a ten-minute break may actually calm them down enough to feed better and speed up the overall feed time.

A pacifier often helps if they are hungry, tired or in pain from wind as they get the comfort from sucking but nothing going down into the stomach to exacerbate the wind problem. Once calm, you can resume winding.

Atmosphere

This can be tricky to identify sometimes, as the adults may not be openly aware of a stressful atmosphere because they are tired or arguing themselves but it can affect sensitive babies, especially if they are already tired, hungry or upset. In fact, it can be the baby's crying that is causing stress and tension in the adults, which then feeds back into the baby, making it worse.

If you feel this might be the problem, you can try handing baby over to someone else, which can make an instant difference. I once went to an emergency job where the husband was away and mum and grandma were looking after baby. When I arrived, they had experienced a difficult couple of days and baby was screaming at full volume and being passed from mum to grandma and back again to no effect, but when baby was passed to me she instantly stopped crying.

Truthfully I didn't know whether they wanted to hug me or hit me! That could have been a wonderful moment for claiming to be a 'magical baby whisperer', but I didn't have the heart, and explained that the three of them had been feeding off a vicious circle of stress and anxiety and when held by someone confident and calm, baby felt the difference and stopped crying long enough to calm down.

If there is no one else to pass baby to, then you have to find a way to calm or de-stress yourself. This may be as simple as putting baby down somewhere safe, getting as far away as possible with as many doors between you and them and just breathing or talking to yourself out loud, giving voice to your stress or distress, which can help externalise it (rather than keeping it bottled up inside).

I often use calming music in this situation, and I find it helps both myself and the baby if I hold baby and dance slowly round the room. I have a couple of 'go to' albums on my phone, my favourite being *Jazz for Babies: The Piano Album*. It doesn't really matter what it is as long as it is calming for you, and not something that drives you insane when you hear it repeatedly (like most nursery rhyme albums!).

Use the same music again and again until baby learns to associate it with relaxation and sleep, which makes it a very useful tool to help baby settle in unfamiliar surroundings such as visiting friends or relatives, or on holiday or in hospital.

You could also try slowly and gently bouncing on a yoga or gym ball, either with or without baby, as it really is remarkably effective at stress reduction and you get a thigh workout at the same time.

FAMILY ATMOSPHERE Other atmospheres that affect babies can be created by tensions between parents or other family members or siblings or friends, and also by anxiety. I know that the first few weeks with any baby, especially your first, can be a very worrying time, so a certain level of anxiety is normal and doesn't usually bother babies. But prolonged or extreme anxiety can sometimes be a problem for baby as well as for the sufferer.

If the stress is coming from arguing parents, you both need to recognise this fact, without blame, accept that there is a problem and try to fix it. By working through the investigative process, you will learn how to recognise stress and anxiety, trace it to its source and address it by understanding the causes, devising coping strategies and ultimately eliminating it.

Other environmental factors

Other environmental factors that bear consideration are ones which may cause baby to be uncomfortable in any way, such as their position. For example, being in a chair or car seat bends them slightly in half and may apply pressure to their tummies, causing pain if wind is still present or if they are constipated, while lying flat for a reflux baby too soon after a meal can be painful as it makes it harder for the stomach valve to keep the milk and acid down.

Other causes of discomfort include their clothing (too small, too tight or creased), their nappy (the elastic can dig into the skin), nappy rash, the angle of their neck and head, limbs twisted or bent, circulation being stopped by position, fingers and toes trapped in clothing or blankets. This sounds alarming but is easily prevented with a little thought and frequent checks.

Biological states

These are the factors that exist within the baby themselves and include hunger, tiredness, pain and illness – all vitally important yet often overlooked or misinterpreted.

When trying to diagnose a situation, you must be able to recognise all these factors before you can assess accurately what effect they are having on baby.

Hunger

New parents are understandably unsure when trying to interpret the signals baby is giving them.

They may think they should feed their baby whenever they wake up, especially if they want to do demand-feeding, but babies can wake up for many different reasons. They may have wind in their stomach, or may wake when they pass wind or have a bowel movement and then resettle themselves, given time or a cuddle.

Maybe they are just going from a deep sleep to a light sleep, and, if left, will return to a deep sleep; or have had a dream that unsettled them and all they need is a reassuring cuddle or a pat, or a soothing word.

Maybe they simply want to be awake to look around and have a little squeak and will be perfectly happy if left to their own devices. Perhaps they are a little hungry, but not hungry enough to have a good feed, in which case a cuddle may allow them to sleep another half hour, by which time they could be properly hungry and feed well.

> It can be quite stressful standing over a baby waiting to see if they will settle back to sleep, so my tip is to go away and do something to distract yourself for a few moments. I use the time to wash bottles, restock the nappy bag, fold laundry.

It is useful to remember that what babies really need most of the time are good feeds and long, undisturbed periods of sleep, and that unnecessary feeds are going to disrupt this, so you need to be sure that a feed is actually what your baby is signalling for.

DEMAND-FEEDING This is equally true for demand-feeders, where natural stirring noises and movements may be misread as a 'demand' for a feed. The parent's life can then become an unending cycle of feeds every ten or twenty minutes, snacks which don't satisfy the baby and may lead to a great deal of wind and short, broken sleeps which are as bad for baby as they are for us.

Keeping a simple record of what time baby fed, how long they fed for and the amount taken can help you keep track of what is happening and to realise when they might be genuinely hungry or wanting a snack.

The obvious sign that a baby is hungry is when they wake up from a sleep. In some babies this may mean that they stir momentarily but go back to sleep for a few minutes before stirring again, then they may open their eyes and look around, being happy for a few more minutes before starting to make increasingly persistent and urgent noises. This is good, as it gives you plenty of time to wake up in the night and prepare the bottle or yourself.

Other babies, however, go from a deep sleep to an ear-shattering scream in a split second which, while totally normal, can leave you in a state of shock when they do it at night. I have literally found myself on the other side of the room with a bottle in my hand before my eyes were even open and without any memory of how I got there, when woken from a deep sleep!

A more subtle sign may be when they lose their sense of humour, and by this I mean when baby is happy being cuddled or looking around but then gradually or suddenly becomes unhappy or restless.

WHY BABIES SUCK A sleeping or calm baby may also show hunger by making a sucking movement with their lips, but beware: this can be very misleading.

Babies like to suck for a number of reasons, first and foremost because it is their main source of comfort.

A tired baby sucks (breast, pacifier, your finger or their own fingers or thumb) to help them go to sleep, which creates an association between sucking and sleep, leading them sometimes to make a sucking motion when they are feeling tired.

Babies may suck in their dreams or as they change their depth of sleep and they also suck to gain relief from pain or stress so, again, because of the association with relief, they can make the sucking motion if they have wind, are constipated or in any other type of pain.

> You can use the pacifier or a clean finger to help you judge whether baby is serious about wanting a feed. If they refuse the pacifier, or accept it readily but calmly, then they are probably not hungry and can wait a while longer. However, if they latch on and suck vigorously and seem annoyed when you remove it, then they are probably ready for a feed.

Babies have a very strong evolutionary rooting reflex, which means that when their face or head is touched they automatically turn towards the direction of the touch and make a sucking motion especially if bare skin is involved. The function of this is to help them find the nipple for breastfeeding but is so strong in the first few weeks that it can happen at any time, whether the baby is hungry or not, so is *not* a reliable indicator of real hunger.

An equally confusing sucking motion can occur after a feed as a leftover action because they have been sucking for a while and continue to do so. This can lead inexperienced parents to think that their baby is still hungry at the end of a feed, or hungry again after just a few minutes.

After a while you will get used to your own baby's signals and will know when they have really finished a feed, but until then one of the easiest ways to judge their hunger is by giving them either a clean finger or a pacifier to suck on for a few minutes. Another way may be to distract the baby by getting up and walking around, monitoring their behaviour (but make sure nothing is touching the sides of their face, triggering the rooting reflex).

> While a gentle to medium touch on baby's cheek will trigger the rooting reflex, a firm touch seems to cancel it out, so if baby is rooting against your chest or arm, try holding them so that their cheek is pressed quite firmly against your body and keep it there for a few seconds or minutes until they relax.

Tiredness

Parents often underestimate the amount of time a new baby needs to sleep, and the impact that lack of sleep may have on all aspects of baby's life, especially on his ability to feed properly (as seen in the case study in Chapter 1, where baby's lack of sleep reduced his ability to tolerate the presence of wind).

Tiny babies tire very quickly, and in the early days even something as minor as a bout of crying, a bath, a medical examination, a clothes change or a walk in the fresh air can exhaust them to the point where they need sleep more than they need food. If this is the case, they may be so sleepy that they are unwilling even to try to feed, or if they do, very quickly fall asleep again.

> In the first few weeks you can use those things that tire a baby out to your own advantage by including them in baby's routine just before you want them to sleep. I often use walks and baths to nudge babies over into sleep when I am devising routines.

Your baby may be tired yet still find it hard to settle to sleep for various reasons. Sometimes it is because they haven't had enough to eat or have not been sufficiently winded; or that they are being disturbed by handling or family goings-on, i.e. interesting or loud noises, lights, smells or atmosphere. Another problem may be that though they are tired, they need help getting off to sleep with cuddles, pats or rocking, and either the parents or carers haven't realised baby is trying to go to sleep or are busy with other things or caring for siblings or doing the school run.

A tired baby is not always a problem, but sometimes they can get upset and out of sorts and end up crying or screaming, which can be mistaken for a need for something else. The easiest way to eliminate tiredness as the cause of crying is to think about how much sleep they have had so far during the day, and also since the last feed.

In Chapter 3, we will go into more detail about the importance of monitoring what the baby is doing during the day and night, especially in the first few weeks. This will help you get to know your baby so you will soon know how much sleep they need to remain happy and content, which varies to a huge extent from baby to baby and is something no book or expert can tell you.

FALLING ASLEEP DURING FEEDS Apart from crying, another sign that a baby is tired is if they are falling asleep during feeds. They drink just enough milk to take the edge off their hunger, then they fall asleep, sometimes even before you get a chance to wind them, and they may be almost impossible to wake up again. The knock-on effect of this is that they have not taken enough food to keep them asleep for the two or three hours until the next feed, and so wake up hungry again after a short time.

It may not be a problem if you are demand-feeding or have only one child, but it can be disastrous if you are trying for a routine, have something you wanted to do between feeds or have other children who need feeding, attention or transporting to activities.

Changing baby's nappy in the middle of a feed is a great way to wake them up and a good opportunity for winding, so use it strategically as part of your feeding plan.

If baby is tired but not irritable, then I put effort into waking them up until they get enough food to allow them to sleep for a decent length of time. I generally set aside a whole hour for the baby's feed, which gives me plenty of time to go through the process of feeding, winding, waking and calming as required. I know some babies are lovely easy feeders and don't usually need a full hour, but if you mentally reserve the hour as being your baby's time to feed, it can help you avoid the trap of becoming impatient or resentful if feeding drags on.

This can also help if you have a sleepy or a small baby who is difficult to wake. It is tempting to let them sleep and declare the feed over, but it can make a big difference to their milk intake over twenty-four hours if you persist and give them the whole hour.

> If your baby is really difficult to wake, try fast-running warm water over their bare feet.

Obviously if your baby is a good weight, feeds quickly and then settles or sleeps contentedly until the next feed, then that is just their way and you don't need to keep waking them. Remember though that if they do ever have a long or difficult feed, this is totally normal; let them have the full hour.

Another sign of tiredness may be that baby feeds well but gets irritated when you are trying to wind them or change their nappy.

All they really want to do is go to sleep, and they get annoyed when you disturb them and so cry, whinge, grumble or, if they are very tired, get seriously upset and scream.

The best way to head this off is to try to ensure that baby has at least one hour's solid sleep before each feed. I always endeavour to make this a priority, and it works very well. If they have had a feed but are then tired and upset and you still need to wind them, there are some relaxing, passive methods to winding which I explain in Chapter 6, which are less likely to annoy a tired baby.

Pain

The most frequent cause of pain in a baby is wind, but the presence of wind can be difficult to diagnose because the symptoms the baby shows are very similar to many other problems. One good way to check is to offer baby a pacifier or clean finger to suck (little finger placed upside down with nail resting on the tongue and soft pad facing upwards). If they suck strongly without obvious discomfort but get upset when offered the breast or bottle, then wind is the likely culprit.

This is because milk going down into a stomach with wind in it will make the pain worse, either by further distending the already overstretched stomach or by causing the problematic bubble to move to an even more painful place, whereas the sucking from the pacifier doesn't affect the stomach in any way but just provides comfort. (This is why the baby in the case study in Chapter 1 was initially eager to get back on the breast but came off again very quickly.)

Although there are close similarities between a baby crying with wind and a baby crying for other reasons, there are a few other clues that may help you with a diagnosis.

The baby, at first feeding well, may then begin to wriggle a little, or may lose the easy breathe-suck-swallow rhythm and start to gasp or feed in short bursts.

This is due to the wind beginning to build up in the stomach, making baby uncomfortable and disturbing their concentration, and is usually a good signal that the feed needs to be halted while you try to help baby burp.

A very common problem occurs when parents get some burps out of the baby and assume that all the wind is gone and then try to continue with the feed. However, while some babies get little wind, others can get the most inexplicably huge amounts, which can take great efforts to dislodge and can interrupt the feed until the issue is resolved.

It is usually easy to recognise when a baby still has wind, as they either refuse to go back onto the breast or bottle, or go back on but are still restless and wriggling.

This can sometimes be misinterpreted as a sign that the baby has had enough to drink, but a full, non-windy baby is usually calm and sleepy rather than wriggly and squeaky. In this case, it is better to stop feeding and concentrate on winding until baby can calmly go back to feeding.

If a baby is in severe pain from wind, they will cry and scream, sometimes inconsolably, in which case it becomes obvious and you can stop and focus on it until the wind comes up.

> One fairly reliable symptom of wind is when a calm or sleeping baby very suddenly shows signs of distress, often with sudden kicking out of the legs or bringing legs up towards the chest at the same time as crying or yelping sharply.

INTESTINAL WIND Wind in the stomach can be brought up by the baby with help from parents, but if the wind has passed through the stomach and is in the **intestines**, there is no way of getting it out until the baby passes it naturally.

Symptoms of this may be exactly the same as wind in the stomach so can be very hard to diagnose, but if you keep winding for what feels like forever and nothing comes up but baby is still distressed, then it could be down to intestinal wind. If this is the case, the only thing you can do is to try to comfort or distract baby (depending on their age), and make them as comfortable as possible until nature takes its course.

It is worth using a pacifier in this situation, as it will give baby relief from pain but will also go some way to stimulating the digestive system and speed up the passing of wind without the added pressure from more milk, which may cause more pain. Other ways of managing this situation will be explored in Chapter 6.

Leaving baby lying face down on your lap with their abdomen directly over your thigh and their legs dangling down for five or ten minutes can often provide enough gentle pressure, in conjunction with movement from baby's own breathing, to help them pass wind.

ENVIRONMENTAL PAIN If your baby seems comfortable wherever they are but then suddenly starts to grumble or complain, it is worth giving them a quick check over to make sure there is nothing external causing the pain such as the environmental factors already discussed, for example a twisted limb, tight clothing, a finger caught in the blanket or ear bent backward (common in feeding positions).

ILLNESS Pain from illness can be equally difficult to diagnose as it is generally expressed by crying, just like most of the other potential problems, so in this case it helps to look at the overall picture of the baby's behaviour coupled with your own knowledge of what is normal for your baby.

Assuming your baby is over a month old and you have had a chance to get to know them, you might look for a change in their behaviour over a period of a few hours or the day so far.

Are they less hungry than usual? Less tolerant of wind or noise or handling? Are they crying more than usual, or grizzling? More sleepy than usual?

You can also check their temperature and keep an eye on their nappy for signs of diarrhoea, and check their whole body for rashes.

Crying can raise a baby's temperature, so to get an accurate reading it is always a good idea, if possible, to wait ten minutes after baby has stopped crying before using a thermometer unless you suspect serious illness, in which case seek medical help immediately.

If a baby is coming down with a cold, they can seem uncomfortable and not themselves for twenty-four hours or more before other, more obvious symptoms appear. This discomfort can be caused by aching muscles, sore throat and headache, just like an adult would feel, and if not suffering severe distress, the baby can be comforted by extra cuddles, pacifiers, warm baths (bathing with parents is especially nice for them as they can still be cuddled), or distractions such as walks in the pram or in a sling, or music and mobiles.

The best thing for a sick baby is sleep, as this takes all the stress off their bodies, allowing them to focus their energy towards fighting the illness, so try to make sure they get as much sleep as possible.

Obviously if you feel your baby is in pain or distress, or you are in any way worried, then seek medical advice as soon as possible, especially if they are under eight weeks old or others in the household are ill, or have been in contact with sick adults or children.

TONGUE TIE Nowadays a common assumption if there are breastfeeding issues is that baby has a tongue tie, where the small thin strip of skin that attaches the tongue to the bottom of the mouth extends too far down the tongue towards the tip. This can prevent the tongue from being able to make the correct shape around the nipple or teat in order to create efficient suction and can cause discomfort and frustration.

If this is the case, then getting it snipped can make a marked difference. However, conversations with paediatricians, midwives and doctors have led me to believe that tongue tie is frequently overdiagnosed, especially in breastfeeding cases. This leads to tongues being unnecessarily snipped when in fact perseverance, expert guidance and support are what is needed (but it is still worth getting baby checked out if you are worried).

CONSTIPATION One final and fairly common source of pain can be from constipation, and can happen in breastfed and bottle-fed babies alike.

It is common for baby's poos to be less frequent as they go through a growth spurt or illness because the body is retaining food longer in order to extract more nutrients, so as long as they are not showing signs of discomfort or pain it is fine to leave them for two or three days.

A constipated baby can be generally unhappy, but can also show specific signs such as being able to feed calmly but then starting to wriggle and cry as the feed progresses, which doesn't ease even after winding.

This is because the milk from the feed is stimulating the bowels, which increases pressure around the blockage. If you suspect this may be the problem, try to get baby as calm as possible then very gently apply gradual pressure to the lower abdomen and watch baby's reaction. If they tense up and cry it could well be constipation.

Some people advise doing tummy massage and cycling baby's legs, but having suffered this way myself as an adult I think I would be wary of causing more pain. I know massage may help speed up the passage of the faecal blockage, but please use your judgement carefully and stop if you think you are making it worse.

> My own favourite cure for constipation is to give baby no more than 30ml of sugar water (½ tsp sugar dissolved in 30ml boiled, cooled water) preferably on an empty stomach. This usually works within two to five hours, without causing extra pain.

Temperament

Historically the new baby's personality has been considered of little importance, which has led to a uniform approach and an outbreak of one-size-fits-all routines which work for some babies but not for others.

In more recent times there have been moves towards recognising the importance of baby's personality, which is an improvement, but often the baby is defined as being of one particular personality type. Experience has taught me that it is not quite as simple as that, because your baby is not born with a personality; they are born with a temperament, and there is a very important difference.

This is a very complicated subject, but the simplified version is that your baby will come into the world with a set of genetic traits that together create your baby's temperament. This includes their own particular need for sleep and food; their threshold for boredom, patience, fear or insecurity; their pain tolerance; their ability to return to a calm state after an upset; their tactile preferences and sense of humour.

> Before baby is born, it can be quite a good idea for the parents to make a list of their own character traits, both good and bad. This can help you recognise similar traits in your baby, enabling you to get to know them more quickly.

From the moment the baby is born these traits will be affected, for better or worse, by their immediate environment, by the parenting they receive and, later, by their life experiences. This process of interaction is what will gradually, over the years, shape the baby's, child's and adult's personality.

As soon as this interaction begins there is the potential for understanding, acceptance, guidance and personality growth, but also for misunderstanding, pigeonholing, judgement and harm, depending on the attitudes of the parents and immediate carers.

The most important thing for you to remember is that your baby is an individual and must be treated as such, with compassion, understanding, acceptance and respect.

It will help you greatly if you take the time to get to know your baby's character traits, and to do this you need to be observant, keep an open mind and be non-judgemental.

Observation

Watching babies is very easy and enjoyable, but the difference between that and *observing* is down to thinking about what you are seeing. For instance, noticing something about your baby's behaviour is good, but even better is thinking about what this may be revealing about them.

The fact that a baby wakes and immediately screams for a feed may tell you something about their patience levels, while a baby that gets very upset when they have wind may be indicating a low pain tolerance. Sometimes what you observe may indicate more than one temperament trait. For example, a baby that wakes frequently may be revealing something about their hunger levels, noise sensitivity, insecurity, pain tolerance or sleep requirements, and the only way to learn more is to think about what the baby is doing in relation to everything else around them.

Ask yourself, is this their normal behaviour? When did they last feed? Did I wind them properly? Might they be reacting to sudden noises? How many times have they slept today and for how long? Asking these sorts of questions once may not reveal much, but if you ask them repeatedly you will begin to see a pattern that could give you valuable insight into their temperament, especially if you record your observations, because the patterns then become much easier to see.

Any time you are puzzled by your baby's behaviour, try keeping a simple record of when it occurs and what else is going on at the time. This can help to give you insight into what might be causing it.

Thresholds

Once you start to recognise your baby's temperament, you can use this knowledge to solve problems, plan ahead and create an effective care routine that meets their needs and yours. However, I would like to caution you against using this knowledge to pigeonhole your baby or judge them.

I explained to one set of parents that their baby had a low pain threshold, especially for wind, and the father's first comment was that he didn't want his son to be a crybaby. This was a casual comment, not meant to be unkind, but to start thinking of his child in this way could lead him to label his child unfairly and perhaps be dismissive or judgemental of any future crying.

I explained how that sort of thinking could prove very unhelpful for both the parents and the child, and that a more productive response would be to accept the trait, recognise that the baby needs his understanding and that it was up to his parents to take this into account when they fed and winded him and to find ways to make his life easier.

The life of a new baby is very confusing and stressful, and they have no understanding of what is happening to them and no coping mechanisms, so their reactions are often much more extreme than that of an older child or an adult. Where a hungry baby will scream for food until it is fed, a hungry child of seven will ask for food, go and get a snack or understand that they have to wait.

Equally, a baby with a low pain tolerance will gradually learn not to panic when they are in pain, will be able to tell you where it hurts, understand when you explain what is happening and believe you when you tell them it will stop. They will learn to cope without crying and screaming much faster and more effectively with accepting, supportive, non-judgemental parenting guidance.

Remember, the character traits they are born with are just the starting point; how their personality progresses and develops will be largely down to their parents or carers.

Emotional response

In the diagram at the start of this chapter, you can see that there is a second box labelled Emotional Response beneath the Temperament box. This is very important.

Take two hungry babies that are both being fed (environmental factor), and that both get the same amount of wind in their stomach (biological state). If we believe that babies are all the same, we might expect both babies to react the same way. However, in reality the environmental and biological factors are also interacting with each baby's individual temperament.

A baby with a *high pain tolerance* may just wriggle and grunt and carry on with the feed, taking enough milk to assuage his initial hunger. This means he is content enough to stay calm when winded, will burp more easily and be relaxed enough to continue the feed until he is no longer hungry.

A baby with a *low pain tolerance* may become upset at the wind in his stomach much quicker than the first baby and be unable to take in more food, even though he is still very hungry. The pain and the hunger act together to make him so unhappy he can neither relax enough to be winded and relieved of the pain, nor feed more to relieve the hunger, which is too much for him to cope with and causes an emotional reaction.

He becomes so upset that he can do nothing but scream his pain and frustration, and the only way for this to change is by having environmental input from the parents or carers. They need to recognise the problem, calm or distract the baby so that winding can take place, which will then reduce the pain, and allow the feed to continue.

Once this character trait is known about, the parents or carers can use the knowledge to devise strategies to help prevent the problem from escalating. This may mean finding a bottle or teat that prevents so much wind being swallowed in the first place; feeding the baby before they get too hungry; stopping the feed to wind more frequently; making sure baby is well rested and winded before the feed; keeping things calm and quiet during the feed to help prevent the baby getting overstressed, or distracting baby during the feed.

If you know your baby is highly sensitive to wind and gets worked up easily, it might be worth trying to start the feed before your baby is properly awake. This would ensure that the first, hungriest, 'gulpiest' part of the feed takes place with baby half asleep when they should, in theory, feed more calmly and take in less wind.

It is also important to realise that your baby's reactions may differ on a daily or even hourly basis depending on the interaction between their environment, their biology and their temperament that is occurring at that particular moment in time.

In essence, you cannot assume that they will react in the same way they did yesterday or even two hours ago. You have to be able to recognise what is happening now and deal with the baby that is in front of you.

Understanding exactly what the environmental and biological factors are, and how they can affect your baby's temperament at any given time, in any situation, is the key to being able to meet all their needs and become confident, competent parents.

3.

Essential record-keeping

Everything I advise parents to do is based on the idea that parenting should be as simple and uncomplicated as possible, so the fact that I am now going to encourage you to keep written records may seem counter-intuitive. In fact, keeping simple records could make your life a lot easier.

When you have your first baby, everything is so new and exciting and stressful that every little thing baby does seems to be etching itself on your brain, never to be forgotten. But as the hours and days go by with frequent feeds, nappy changes, broken sleep and so many new experiences, your brain will become overloaded and unable to recall accurately what has been happening. This leads to confusion and misunderstanding, making it very difficult to figure out what is causing a particular problem.

Whenever I go to new clients, I always suggest we keep some sort of record for this very reason, and also because they can see clearly what I am doing with their baby, plus it is nice to have as a keepsake.

I have come across parents who want to record absolutely everything baby does as a detailed diary, which of course I am happy to do. But I also keep my own records, which are much

57

simpler and more workmanlike, as it is easy for the important information to get lost in the narrative of a detailed journal.

Baby records

The main details needed to help sort problems and adjust routines include: time of feed; duration of feed if breastfeeding, or amount of milk taken if bottle-feeding; time of sleep; length of sleep; and when baby poos. You can add other information if you are facing a particular problem: for instance, if you are trying to discover why your baby cries, it may be useful to keep a note of when they cry and what is happening at the time.

There are many different ways of arranging and recording this information, and there are some ready-printed diaries available with different sections to write in and boxes to tick, but I tend to find the formats restrictive for whatever it is I am trying to record. Personally I prefer a blank A5 lined notebook, and you can get some with very attractive covers.

> Get into the habit of leaving the book and pen in the same place, so that you or your partner or another carer can access it easily in order to record or check details.

The information needs to be easy to see, and I organise it so that a tired eye can scan down the page and access very easily whatever details they need.

Date	Time	Nappy	Feed	Sleep
Tuesday 10 June	7.10	P	120ml/4oz	
	8.30			40 mins (wind)
	9.25			35 mins
	10.00	W	100ml/3.5oz	
	10.45			2 hrs (deep)
	12.00	P	100ml/3.5oz	
	13.30			2 hrs (restless)
	15.00	P	100ml/3.5oz	

From this example, you can see how easy it is to scan down the page and find exactly how much baby had to drink, when they slept and when they had a dirty nappy (P denotes poo and W denotes wee). I also added a little extra information about quality of sleep and reason for waking, as in this case I was trying to work out a way to adjust sleep patterns to accommodate a family outing.

If you were curious about how a pacifier was affecting baby's sleep, you could note how many times you had to replace it during a nap, or when baby slept deeply and soundly and perhaps whether they were swaddled or not.

You could easily scan down to check if baby could possibly be constipated, or if restless sleep coincided with siblings' noisy play date downstairs.

You can also see that baby seems hungrier in the morning, or that they sleep more deeply in the afternoon, which might be useful to know if you are wondering which daytime nap to drop first.

If you were wondering whether your baby has reflux, you could add another column to record when they were sick and how much, e.g. V++ for big vomit, V- for a small vomit, and whether they were upright at the time or lying down, or when baby was most distressed (often very useful information to show a GP or reflux specialist if seeking a diagnosis).

Parental or family records

You can also use the journal to keep track of other things, such as you and your partner's moods. You could add a column to keep track of when you felt depressed, anxious or stressed, and note who was present and what was happening, which could give an insight into potential triggers. Remember, this process can be used to investigate every aspect of parenting, not just what is going on with baby.

The parents are often in need of as much help, and are deserving of as much consideration, as the baby. The health of the family unit is vital, whether it is made up of a single parent, two parents, one child or ten.

I would advise some sort of basic record-keeping at least for baby's first six weeks, as this is when life can seem the most tiring and confusing, but be careful not to make it so complicated that you cannot easily scan down the page to find information.

To counter this tendency to clutter the diary with too much note-making, I sometimes keep two separate diaries: one for facts, and the other for stories about baby's other habits or milestones, or I do what one of my clients came up with and write information on one page and the stories on the facing page, so that everything is kept together but is easily accessible.

Once your baby is in whatever routine you want, or you are

happy with the way everything is going, you can stop, because you can always restart if you sense a problem or have a particular issue you want to address.

In some instances, you might find that keeping a diary for a few days highlights the fact that there isn't really a problem in the first place. One of my clients was worried that baby had started drinking less than normal on some feeds, so I advised her to keep the diary for three full days, and we realised that baby was taking more at two feeds and less at four, but that over a twenty-four-hour period the milk intake was actually the same.

Another client spotted in the diary that baby was drinking less and sleeping more, so worried that she was ill, but looking back over the previous week I was able to point out that baby had seemed extra-hungry and had drunk quite a lot more. I reminded her that baby was the right age for a growth spurt and that this was a very normal pattern, and over the next week she could see that baby returned to her previous pattern and stopped worrying.

Don't worry if your baby seems unusually sleepy after a growth spurt. This is totally normal, and is just a sign that their body is working a bit harder to utilise all the extra milk and do some growing.

Anxiety

It is totally normal for new parents to worry about their baby, and in this constantly anxious state it is common for them to be watching and looking for any signs of problems. When I come across this, I never dismiss their fears or tell them they are being silly or paranoid, because I understand how real that fear is. Instead I reassure them with information, and recount examples from previous clients, and I back this up with real, tangible proof from their own diary.

A word of warning: very occasionally I come across a situation where an anxious parent becomes fixated on record-keeping to an unhealthy degree, noting absolutely everything down to each and every millilitre of milk, and in one case even weighing the wet nappies, even though baby was a good weight and had no health issues.

As I have already stated, a parent's fears and worries should never be dismissed. In these cases I go along with their record-keeping for two to three days until I have had time to assess the situation properly, and then we have a talk and I try to explain how the fixation is reinforcing the anxiety instead of allaying it.

My suggestion is to attempt to face the anxiety and tackle it rather than ignoring it or just dismissing it as 'a new parent thing'. I offer practical ideas such as gradually weaning the parent off their anxious habit, perhaps starting by weighing only every other nappy, or rounding milk intake up or down to nearest 5ml or 10ml, or by keeping my own diary and using it to demonstrate on a daily basis how this provides us with the information we really need.

I also find it greatly helps anxious parents to get the baby into a routine as soon as possible, to bring in an element of predictability which in itself has a calming effect for many parents.

Whether you use my method or develop your own, a diary or log of some sort will be an invaluable tool during the first few weeks of parenthood, so it is worth investing some time and thought in the practice.

Remember, being a parent of a new baby is an extremely stressful and unpredictable experience, and responding to this feeling of lack of control by obsessing over details is a very common reaction. Recognise it for what it is and try to find some way of relaxing about it. Be as patient and understanding towards yourself as you would be with a friend in the same situation.

4.

How to carry out your own investigation

How you begin an investigation depends very much on what sort of problem you are facing. I will talk more about pre-emptive planning in Chapter 5, but for now I will focus on more immediate problems.

The most helpful state for any investigation is one in which you have peace and quiet and time to think, which is not usually too difficult to organise if it is a non-urgent problem such as adjusting routines or feed and sleep patterns, or perhaps working from a general feeling of something not being quite right.

Find time to think

Finding a moment to think will be much more difficult if you are facing a more urgent problem – you are an exhausted parent, facing a screaming baby and rampaging siblings. In this situation you can use some sort of intervention to give yourself time to breathe and to think.

This might involve emergency measures, such as sitting siblings in front of a television or iPad or sending them out with friends or relatives for an afternoon, or waiting until they are in bed. It might mean finding a way to quieten baby with a pacifier/swaddle/sling, or taking a walk outside with the pram.

Once you have created your space and time to think, you will need to find pen and paper, or some way of recording your thoughts, because writing things down is a very effective way of taking control of whatever is bothering you.

The sort of tiredness that results from broken sleep has a particular way of fracturing your thought processes, making thinking straight very difficult and the memory unreliable. Myself and my clients have found jotting down thoughts and ideas to be invaluable to problem-solving.

The next thing to do is to take a step back emotionally.

I know from personal experience that this is easier said than done, but you should try to let go of blame or guilt and all the other negative emotions that assail struggling parents. Try to think about the situation as a knot that needs untangling rather than as a parenting fail. The calmer you are, the easier it will be for you to find the 'end' you need to begin the untangling process.

AIM process – Assess, Investigate and Modify: defining the problem

In the past when I was taking clients through the problem-solving process I used phrases such as 'seeing what is really happening, what is really there'; 'figure out what the problem is and then figure out what to do about it'. When I came to design the process for the purposes of this book, I wanted to try to make things clearer and more concise, and it was at this point that I came across a man called Dr Jade Teta, a health and fitness expert in the US, whose programmes I love because they follow the same principles as my own of becoming a detective to solve problems. He encourages his clients to solve their own metabolic challenges, finding their own unique solutions by using the acronym **AIM**: Assess, Investigate, Modify, which sums up exactly what I intend to teach you to do. With Dr Teta's blessing, I am adopting that same acronym.

Define the problem

This is a vital part of your investigation, because it will give you your starting point, the end of the knot which you can then start to untangle.

Start by asking yourself, 'What is the problem?'

The answer to this might be relatively straightforward and easily identifiable, for example:

- baby won't sleep in their moses basket
- baby won't sleep for more than twenty minutes
- the feeds are a nightmare and take over an hour and a half each time
- I can't wind baby properly
- baby is sick a lot
- baby won't play by themselves
- the routine is all wrong for my other children
- I want to have more flexibility in my routine

But there can also be more complex, less easily defined problems for you, such as general feelings of inadequacy, feeling unhappy or depressed, being exhausted, not enjoying baby or being a parent, feeling out of control or that your partner is a better parent than you are, that people are criticising or judging you or that somehow the way you are doing things doesn't feel right. In this case, write down all the things that are bothering you and see if one item stands out that is causing more worry than any of the others. Or prioritise the list, writing down issues in order of difficulty; or try to condense it into one short sentence. This activity can help you focus.

Phase 1: Assessment (what?)

Once you know exactly what your problem is, you can go ahead and start **Assessing** the situation, by asking yourself or each other questions about what is happening, relating them back to the factors we discussed in Chapter 2 that may be affecting your baby and yourselves, namely **environmental factors**, **biological states** and **temperament**.

Start by thinking about the last time the problem or the difficult feeling occurred. Fix it clearly in your head and describe that time with as much detail as possible so that you can refer back to it. Then ask yourselves *exactly* what was happening, using the following five questions. Don't worry about why or how it happened; just concentrate on writing down *what happened*.

1 *Where were you and baby?*
Indoors or outdoors? At home, or somewhere else? Which room were you in? Which chair/bed/sofa were you sitting on?

2 *Who else was there?*
Just you and baby? Your partner? Friend/relative/health professional/other children?

3 *What was your environment like?*
Describe noise, light, temperature, air movement, activity, atmosphere.

4 *How were you feeling?*
Were you exhausted, hungry, in pain, ill, stressed, frustrated, relaxed, happy, calm, comfortable? Were you feeling positive, negative, confident, anxious, angry, sad, confused?

5 *How was baby behaving?*
Upset, e.g. crying, screaming? Uncomfortable, e.g. wriggling, stiffening body, thrashing limbs? Was baby calm and relaxed? Focused? Distracted?

To help illustrate the **Assessment** process, I have worked through two different problems, below, to demonstrate some of the possible questions and their answers, which we can then use to explore the **Investigate** and **Modify** phases of the investigation.

EXAMPLE PROBLEM A:

the feeds are a nightmare

First baby, six weeks old, bottle-fed

WHAT HAPPENED? Bottle feed at 11 a.m. today

- Baby was awake and crying/screaming
- Started feeding as if he was starving and gobbled milk quickly
- Fed for two minutes, then started coughing/spluttering
- Winded for two minutes but had to give up as baby was screaming for more food
- Fed for about five minutes, still greedily. Calmed down a little but gradually started to wriggle and squirm
- Wriggling increased with baby coming off the teat more frequently until he stopped feeding altogether
- Tried to wind again, but baby was struggling and very uncomfortable. He did two big burps and seemed calmer, so I resumed the feed
- Baby fed but was very wriggly; was on and off the bottle for the rest of the feed (over an hour and a half altogether)
- Winded again but only got two small burps before baby fell asleep, so swaddled him and put him down in moses basket
- He woke after five minutes, I winded him then put him back down to sleep but he woke several times over the next two hours for more winding

Now we have the details, we can apply our five questions:

1 *Where were you and baby?*
Living room, on sofa

2 *Who else was there?*
No one

3 *What was your environment like?*
Average – daylight, television on quietly

4 *How were you feeling?*
Tired
Apprehensive before feed
Very rushed when he was screaming for his bottle
Dreaded the wriggling starting
Frustrated, annoyed and upset throughout feed
Hopeless and a failure after feed. Very disheartened. Like I
should be able to do such a basic thing

5 *How was baby behaving?*
Upset before feed – crying/screaming
Frantic at the start of the feed
Impatient during the rest of the feed
Uncomfortable – wriggling and frequently coming off the
teat
Unsettled in sleep afterwards

This presents a very clear picture of a bad feed, but to give us some clues and a basis for comparison later, it would be useful to try to think of a feed that went better and follow the same process.

WHAT HAPPENED? 11 p.m. feed

- Picked baby up as soon as he stirred
- Started feed calmly and fed for 15 minutes before wriggling began
- Continued feeding for 10 minutes before stopping
- Winded fairly calmly, burping three times
- Restarted feed. Fed slowly for 10 minutes
- Nappy change to wake him, two more burps
- Fed sleepily for 10 minutes, then fell asleep
- Winded while asleep, over my shoulder. Burped once, swaddled, then put down to sleep
- Slept soundly for four hours

Now apply the five questions:

1 *Where were you and baby?*
Bedroom (in bed)

2 *Who else was there?*
No one

3 *What was your environment like?*
Quiet, calm, low light

4 *How were you feeling?*
Very tired but fairly calm
Comfortable
Less apprehensive but still a bit on edge
Relieved day is nearly over

5 *How was baby behaving?*
Calm and relaxed for most of feed

Became uncomfortable towards middle of feed but calmed
again
Very settled once asleep

I hope you can see that by using the five questions, we are creating order out of chaos, arranging the information in such a
way that it becomes a lot easier to see exactly what is happening.
It also makes it easier to compare one situation with another
when we begin investigating, which we will do in the next phase.

This was a very specific problem, but the process works on
much less easily defined problems.

In the next example, we ask the same questions but apply them
to a much broader picture.

EXAMPLE PROBLEM B:
everything is falling apart and I feel useless

First baby, four weeks old

WHAT IS HAPPENING?

- Baby has no routine and eats and sleeps at different times
  every day
- Baby sleeps more in the day and wakes more at night
- No problems breastfeeding and plenty of milk, but feeds
  take a long time
- Never seem to get anything done
- Always tired
- Feel rushed and anxious when leaving the house
- Get stressed when visitors come, feel inadequate and can't
  wait for them to go

- Feel like people are disapproving/judging me
- Partner only helps when I'm really stressed and gets angry when I am upset
- Not enjoying baby and feel guilty about that
- Feel very alone

Now we can apply the five questions to the facts, and organise them to help us see what is happening more clearly.

As this scenario is less specific, we must ask our questions in a slightly different way. We focus on the main problem – in this case the general feeling of things falling apart and being useless – and ask *where* and *when* and *how* things felt worse.

1 *Where were you and baby (when you felt useless)?*
   At home – no specific room
   Out and about – buses, cafés, other houses, park, doctor's surgery, shops

2 *Who else was there?*
   At home – parents, siblings on both sides of the family. Much worse when mother-in-law and sister-in-law were there. Partner too, when he was being unsupportive/ angry
   Out and about – mums from baby group, friends from work, strangers

3 *What was your environment like?*
   At home – worse when levels of noise and activity and clutter were high, and when atmosphere was tense
   Out and about – worse when on public transport and in crowded places where activity and noise were high and personal space compromised

4 *How were you feeling?*

At home:

- tired all the time, even after a sleep
- discomfort, still bleeding quite heavily
- lethargic, diet poor and no exercise
- disorganised/chaotic, nothing gets done
- stressed
- anxious
- depressed
- tearful
- betrayed and let down by partner
- frustrated by inability to cope

Out and about:

- stressed
- panicking
- tearful
- anxious

5 *How was baby behaving?*

Calm, but takes a long time to feed

Sleeps a lot in the day and more awake at night

As with Example A: the feeds are a nightmare, we also need to discover if there are any times when the mother felt things were better – even if only slightly – to allow comparisons, and to help us spot patterns in the investigation phase.

WHAT WAS HAPPENING?

Felt better:
* when I was alone or out of the house (once I got where I was going)
* when baby slept after a feed and I could watch a DVD box set
* when I was out with friends J and D (supportive and understanding)
* when partner had baby and I could have a bath
* out for a walk on my own

It is not as straightforward applying the five questions to this situation, but it is still worth doing to illustrate the differences in situations.

1 *Where were you and baby (when you felt better)?*
At destination when out
In park
In bath (alone)

2 *Who else was there?*
Alone or with friends J and D or when baby was asleep

3 *What was your environment like?*
Quiet
Calm
Fresh air on walk
Plenty of personal space

4 *How were you feeling?*
Calm
Relieved
Supported

5 *How was baby behaving?*
Asleep
Calm in pram

These two scenarios are both very different, but the same questions are being asked, always referring back to the factors that can affect both yourself and your baby.

These same factors can affect other family members, especially siblings, so you can ask the same questions about them, too, to help get a good idea of what is happening with everyone, and add the results to your notes.

It can be very difficult to describe what is happening without adding reasons or justifications, but keep reminding yourself that you are interested in the 'now' and the rest will come later.

This is the equivalent of the investigators taking pictures of the crime scene, drawing the chalk outline and getting a list of suspects. The investigation has not yet begun.

If you have a partner, it can sometimes be very useful to get them to go through the same process separately, then compare results, as a different perspective can give more insight (just make sure you both understand that there is to be **no blame** involved at any point).

For some people this joint assessment is not an option, either because they are single parents, or have a partner who is not good at this sort of introspection, or because you simply want to get a clearer picture of what is going on in your own head before deciding to involve anyone else. In this case, you will be reliant on your own observations, so writing accurate notes is even more important.

I realise that if you are already struggling to cope, the added note-making and diary-keeping may seem like a chore, but I promise you it will be well worth the effort. Indeed, sometimes just this first stating of facts in the Assessment phase is enough to help people realise what the problem is, and the answer comes immediately.

Phase 2: Investigation (why?)

Having defined our problem and recorded exactly what has been happening, we are now ready to begin the next phase, the **Investigation**.

This is where we start to ask the question 'Why?' and apply it to our observations to try to discover what might be causing or contributing to the problem.

This is also the phase where you may be challenged on a very personal level, perhaps realising that some of what is happening might be as a result of you or your partner's actions, and may open you up to feelings of guilt, blame, failure or inadequacy, which can be very hard to cope with. So be prepared, but don't worry. Once you know and accept whatever is going wrong, you can figure out how to fix it and move forward with your parenting skills with confidence.

PROJECTED FEELINGS Please be aware that it is quite common for people to project their own feelings, beliefs, fears, anxieties and habits onto their babies. In the case study in Chapter 1, the mum had projected her own feelings about how she thought it would feel to be swaddled as an adult onto her baby, assumed her baby would hate it and so deprived herself of an amazingly useful tool which, in the end, proved to be something her baby loved.

Many of these projections arise out of a natural fear of doing something wrong that might harm a baby's long-term mental, emotional or physical health, fears often exacerbated by media and social media scare stories and parenting propaganda. I know how powerful this can be, but please remember that babies are much more resilient than we think, and that it is extremely unlikely you will harm them through everyday interactions.

You need to prepare yourself for this beforehand, and realise that those feelings are experienced by all new parents and are totally normal, but are also unhelpful and potentially destructive.

DEALING WITH EMOTIONS If you do start to feel overwhelmed by more negative emotions, it may help to remind yourself that the reason you are experiencing them is because you care. You care about the health and happiness of your baby, and that is exactly how you will find the strength to work through those feelings to solve the problem – not because you *want* to be a good parent, but because you *already are*!

The most important thing you can do is to focus on being as objective and honest as you can possibly manage, and to cling onto your sense of humour with all your strength because that, more than anything, will help you through.

I love it when we get to this stage, because it is so empowering.

Here is where we tackle the problem head-on and take control.

Here is where we gain insight, and the puzzle starts to make sense, which, especially in seemingly hopeless situations, can be very exciting.

LEADS TO FOLLOW Every detective needs leads to follow and lines of investigation to pursue as they try to uncover what is happening, and we are no different.

I find it helps to keep focused by returning to the things which matter most to your baby: **to be well fed, well rested, relaxed and comfortable**.

To this end, I have devised four very straightforward questions to ask, whenever we sense that something is not right with baby:

1 *Could this be causing my baby to be tired/overtired?*
2 *Could this be causing my baby to be hungry/overly hungry?*
3 *Could this be causing my baby to be stressed/overstimulated?*
4 *Could this be causing my baby to be uncomfortable/in pain?*

We are looking for clues that might explain baby's behaviour, so let's remind ourselves of the possible affecting factors:

ENVIRONMENTAL FACTORS Things that affect baby but that they have no control over: temperature, noise, light, handling, air movement, smells, position, movement (handling) and emotional atmosphere

BIOLOGICAL STATES Internal states that can only be felt by baby. Hunger, thirst, tiredness/overtiredness, insecurity/fear, pain, discomfort, illness

TEMPERAMENT Thresholds for patience, pain, exhaustion, boredom, noise sensitivity, overstimulation, time needed to get wound up and to calm down

EMOTIONAL RESPONSE A result of environmental factors and biological states that act on the temperament, creating either a positive or a negative response from baby

THE IMPORTANCE OF PATTERNS As we begin exploring the situation, an essential thing to bear in mind is that it is observing *patterns* of behaviour that will result in breakthroughs, and by that I mean not only noticing what is happening, but how often it happens and in what circumstances.

As you refer back to your diary and start asking questions, you may begin to notice that every time baby wakes up tired and grumpy you have a bad feed; or that you are more likely to get a good night's sleep when you spend extra time winding baby last thing at night.

You might see a correlation between your stress levels and days when you have multiple visitors; or that you feel less stressed about leaving the house on those days when baby is asleep for an hour before departure time so you don't feel rushed.

TEST YOUR THEORY If you think you see a pattern emerging, use that as a basis for creating a theory and then test it. For example, write down, 'Does my baby always feed better after he has had a good sleep just before the feed?' Then keep your diary again for the next twenty-four hours, paying particular attention to the duration and timing of sleeps.

If your results are not conclusive, then try another twenty-four hours. Not only can this confirm or disprove your theory, it will give you real data that you can use when we go on to the modification phase, because when you start trying to change the routine to improve feeds you will already know that your baby seems to need a bare minimum of an hour's sleep before each feed, and is even better with an hour and a half.

You may think you see a pattern and be ready to act on it, but after testing your theory, find that it was just a fluke. This is not a bad thing, and it doesn't mean you 'got it wrong'. In fact, it is a positive sign that you are being intelligent and open-minded, and, by accepting that you don't always get it right first time, it is great practice for the trial-and-error approach that will be needed in the modification phase. It will also save you time by ruling out certain affecting factors, narrowing your focus down to the most likely causes.

There are no rules to say how long this investigation phase should take. I have used it to figure out a problem in twenty-four hours or less, but sometimes, in more difficult cases, it has taken days or even weeks of repeated observation, diary-keeping and retesting of theories. Have patience, follow the process and you will get there in the end.

To illustrate how an investigation might go, I will return to the examples I used earlier. I have reproduced the Assessment, and annotated in italics some of the possible questions I might ask.

EXAMPLE PROBLEM A:
the feeds are a nightmare

Environmental factors

Where did you feed?
Living room, on sofa.
Were my baby and I both comfortable? Were we still comfortable by the end of the feed?

Light level?
Bright daylight.
Was the light too bright? Could it have been stressing baby when he was screaming, tired and hungry? Might a lower light have been more restful?

Noise level?
Average, television on.
Was the noise level comfortable for baby and I? If we were stressed, could relaxing music have been beneficial?

Other people?
Alone.
Was this a good thing? Might someone to talk to have helped me relax, so reducing a possible stressful atmosphere that might have been affecting my baby? Or is being on my own all I can cope with when experiencing a difficult feed?

Handling level?
Low.
No questions here, as low level of handling was all baby could cope with when tired and hungry.

Atmosphere?
Stressed.
Was my stress feeding back to baby and making the feed worse? If I could find ways to relax myself, might I be better able to cope when things go wrong? Was I prioritising baby over myself and not recognising my own needs?

Biological states

Tired?
Yes, baby woke crying.
Why was baby tired? Did he not get enough sleep after the last feed? How much sleep did he have? How much sleep does he need to be calm for a feed? Did I not put him down early enough? Did I not wind him enough after the last feed? What might have disturbed his sleep? Was he swaddled? If not, might he have benefited from swaddling? If he

had more sleep, might he have started the feed more relaxed? Would this have made a difference to how calmly he fed?

Hungry?
Very.
Why was he so hungry? Did I not feed him enough at the last feed? Was the gap between feeds too long for him? If so, why was the gap too long? Did I forget to feed him? Was I too busy? Was I too tired, and just making the most of every moment he slept?

Pain?
Unknown, but don't think so.
Good.

Ill?
No.
Good.

Temperament

Sensitivity?
Seems quick to get upset and slow to calm down.
Should I have been taking more trouble to prevent him getting upset so he wasn't so stressed at feed times?

Pain tolerance?
Average; doesn't seem overly upset by wind when calm.
Good.

Patience?
Very impatient when hungry.
How could I avoid this becoming an issue?

(Not sure of anything else, as baby is so new.)

WHAT HAPPENED? Bottle feed at 11 a.m. today

Baby was awake and crying/screaming.
I know his biological state was too tired and hungry, but could other environmental factors have been affecting him? The room was quiet, and I don't think the light was too bright, but possibly my own tension could have been affecting him.

Started feeding as if he was starving and gobbled milk quickly.
Would it have helped if I could somehow have slowed his feeding down? Can I think of any time he started the feed more calmly? If he did start the feed calmly, did it make him choke less or make the feed any easier?

Fed for two minutes, then started coughing/choking.
Was he comfortable? Did he have a good seal around the teat with his lips? Was I concentrating on holding the bottle in the right position? He was too hungry for me to slow him down, but could the teat flow have been too fast? The flow doesn't normally bother him, but maybe he just sucks too strongly when very hungry? Does he always choke, or are some feeds better? If so, how did those feeds differ from the difficult ones?

Winded for two minutes but had to give up as baby was screaming for more food.
If I could have calmed him down enough, could I have got some wind out at this stage, and might that have improved the rest of the feed? Can I remember any feeds where he was calmer, and where he brought up wind at this early stage of the feed? In his already stressed state, might my trying to wind him have caused an emotional response by overstimulating an already overtired and overly hungry baby?

Fed for about five minutes, still greedily. Calmed down a little but gradually started to wriggle and squirm.

As he went back to feeding straight away, could I have calmed him until coughing stopped, then restarted the feed without trying to wind him? Was the wriggling caused by wind building up?

Wriggling increased with baby coming off the teat more frequently until he stopped feeding altogether.
Was this due to wind? Was anything else happening around him that might have been distracting him?

Tried to wind again, but baby was struggling and very uncomfortable. He did two big burps and seemed calmer, so I resumed the feed.
Did I leave it too late to wind him? Should I have stopped earlier, rather than wait for him to stop? Was two burps enough? Could I have tried to wind for a bit longer to see if there was more wind? Why didn't I? Was I too stressed and impatient? If so, would it have helped if I had tried to calm myself down?

Baby fed but was very wriggly; was on and off the bottle for the rest of the feed (over an hour and a half altogether).
What was his biological state? Was he just uncomfortable, or was he in pain? Can I tell the difference? Would it help me to make notes to help me decide? Was the wriggling down to wind building up? Should I have stopped him feeding to do more winding? Why didn't I? Was it because I was desperate for the feed to be over because I had had enough? Or because I don't feel confident or effective at winding? Could the wriggling be caused by constipation? When did he last poo?

Winded again but only got two small burps before baby fell asleep, so swaddled him and put him down in his moses basket.
Do I think he'd had enough milk? Could I have tried to feed him again after the two small burps? Had I winded him enough?

He woke after five minutes, I winded him then put him back down to sleep but he woke several times over the next two hours for more winding.

Why did he keep waking? Could it have been due to wind? Should I have tried to wind him more thoroughly? Would that have woken him up to the point where he wouldn't go back down to sleep? Did that thought scare me, because I was exhausted after the feed? Did the dread of the next feed influence the amount of time I was willing to spend winding and resettling because I was desperate for a break myself? Was there anything else that might be causing him to wake? Light? Noise? Temperature? Position? Swaddle (too tight or not tight enough)?

How did you feel?

Apprehensive before feed.
Am I always apprehensive before his feeds? How long have I been feeling like this? How long before feeds does it start?

Very rushed when he was screaming for his bottle.
Why was I rushed? Did I have his bottle ready? If not, why not? Are his feeds on a schedule? Might it help him or me if they were? Was I trying to do other things? Could I have been more organised? Would it help me feel calmer if I was more organised?

Dreaded the wriggling starting.
Is the dread affecting the feed in any way? Is it preventing me from enjoying the feeds?

Frustrated, annoyed and upset throughout feed.
How bad were these feelings, on a scale of 1 to 5? Did they affect the way I managed the feed? Could I have been more patient, or winded more gently, or persisted for longer, or thought more clearly?

everything is falling apart and I feel useless

First baby, four weeks old

Environmental factors

How are things different from your own, pre-baby normality?
Usually fairly tidy, but house now feels very cluttered. Laundry
done but not put away; fridge full of convenience food, not
usual fairly healthy ingredients. Baby stuff everywhere.
*Why has this happened? Why am I so disorganised? Did partner help
with housework before baby? Are they helping now? Has the level of
help increased, stayed the same or decreased?*

Noise?
Very quiet, no television or music but used to have music on all
the time.
*Why aren't I listening to music any more? Could this be affecting my
mood? Am I trying to keep things quiet for baby? Would music disturb
her? Might she enjoy it?*

People?
Friends or family visit every day, so often busy.
*Do I enjoy the visits? Do I invite people, does my partner invite them
or do they invite themselves? Do they stay too long? Do I have any
control over the time or length of visit?*

Atmosphere?
Tense.
*Is it always tense? Does it increase or decrease when partner is home
or when visitors arrive? Is it all visitors who make me feel tense, or
only particular ones? When am I less tense?*

Biological states

Tired?

Yes, all the time, even after a sleep.

Why am I so tired? Does broken sleep affect me more than just fewer hours' sleep? Have I ever been this tired before, maybe after an illness or under some other form of stress? If so, how did I cope with it then? Did I change my diet or level of exercise, or take supplements? Do I take every opportunity to rest when baby is asleep? Do I get off to sleep easily, or lie awake stressing? If so, what do I stress about?

In pain?

Not pain, but discomfort and bleeding still heavy.

Have I talked to anyone about this? If not, could this be contributing to my tiredness and anxiety? Could I be anaemic? Could I have an infection?

Diet?

Chaotic. Forget to eat then eat junk/comfort food. Evening meal is microwaved.

When did this diet change start, before or after the birth? Am I the only one shopping and cooking? What is preventing me from shopping and cooking the food I like? Is it tiredness, lack of personal organisation or being interrupted by visitors or baby? Is it due to feelings of apathy or anxiety? Do I ever feel better at any time of the day? Might I feel better physically if I ate better and more regularly? Could I be needing more calories due to the breastfeeding?

Exercise level?

Poor. Used to walk a lot but rarely go out now.

Why don't I go out any more? Is it the baby's routine, or my own anxiety? How do I think I would feel if I could get more exercise? Am I physically too tired?

Mood?

Always seem either stressed, anxious or depressed. Very tearful.

Are there any times I have felt either significantly better or worse? Might it help to keep a diary for a few days to try to discover particular triggers? Do I already know the triggers? Could I be suffering from postnatal depression? Does this prospect scare me? Have I talked to anyone about this?

Temperament

Normally sensible, calm and organised but can lack confidence if out of comfort zone. Now anxious, confused, disorganised and easily upset. No confidence in anything.

Which of these feelings worries me most? Which might most easily be tackled? Have I encountered any of these feelings before? If so, when did it occur, and how did I cope? Did I receive medical/professional help? If yes, what has stopped me so far from seeking help again?

WHAT IS HAPPENING?

Baby has no routine and eats and sleeps at different times every day.

Why does baby have no routine? Is it a planned parenting approach? Might I feel better if baby was in some sort of a routine so that I knew when she was feeding and sleeping and could plan my day around her? Might this help me get organised and feel more confident and in control? How does my partner feel about this? Do I know how to set up a routine?

Baby sleeps more in the day and wakes more at night.
Why is this the case? When did it start? Is it because I am so tired in the day that I would rather let her sleep, so that I can try to get some chores done? Is it because I feel less stressed if she stays asleep when visitors are here? Did it just sort of happen? Why might she wake more in the night? Could she be hungry? Is my milk supply as good at night as it is in the day? Do I rush the feeds because I want to get back to sleep? Do I spend enough time winding her? Is anything around her moses basket at night disturbing her (e.g. partner's snoring, noise from street, temperature)?

No problems breastfeeding and plenty of milk, but feeds take a long time.
Why do feeds take so long? Is she extra-hungry from long sleeps/gaps between feeds? Might it help if I give her more breaks and wake her up a bit with winding or nappy changes? Am I just too tired to be more proactive during the feed?

Never seem to get anything done.
Is this down to tiredness, lack of organisation, apathy? Am I trying to do too much and overextending myself? Have things got so out of hand that it's impossible to catch up so I just leave chores undone? Could partner help more? Could we afford some paid help? Could any family member help at all?

Always tired.
Would I be able to cope better if I was less tired? How much of the tiredness is mental and how much is physical? Does partner ever give me a night off? If not, why not? Is it because they won't, or because I won't let them? Do I have confidence in their baby skills? Could I relax enough for them to do night feeds if I express, even if it is one night a week?

Feel rushed and anxious when leaving the house.

Is this general anxiety about leaving the house? Have I ever felt any-thing like this before? Do I feel the same anxiety if I leave the house on my own, or just with baby? Am I giving myself enough time to get ready? Is the lack of a routine for baby making this worse? Am I happy breastfeeding when out of the house, or am I trying to make sure she is fed before I leave? Could I express milk and give her a bottle when out? Do I feel any better when I am on my way to meet my favourite friends?

Get stressed when visitors come, feel inadequate and can't wait for them to go.

Are my guests sympathetic or supporting? Am I relaxed with any visitors, or are they all stressing me? Is there a particular number of visitors per day or per week that I think I could cope with? Would I feel lonely without company, or relieved? Would it help to be able to set the time and duration of the visit? Am I happy breastfeeding in front of visitors, or is the stress of trying to avoid that making me more stressed?

Feel like people are disapproving/judging me.

Could I be imagining the disapproval, or are they really criticising me? Is anyone actually voicing criticism, implying it or doing it with looks? Is there anything in particular they are judging me about? Could I be oversensitive because of hormones or being so tired? Does my partner support me in company, or join in the criticism (even if in jest)? Does anyone ever offer to help in any way? If so, do I accept the help, or pretend I don't need it? Do they know I am struggling, or am I hiding it too well? Is the anxiety being made worse by spending too much time on Facebook and reading people criticising each other?

Partner only helps when I'm really stressed and gets angry when I am upset.

Is this normal behaviour? Did we discuss them helping when I was pregnant? Can we sit down and talk about it now? Could they be feeling helpless and inadequate themselves? If they offer to help, do I let them get on with it or criticise or expect them to do it the way I do? Am I giving them enough time just to be with the baby, or am I trying to do it all myself? Could my partner be feeling left out and neglected?

Am I so busy with baby that I ignore them? Could I try talking to them and asking for help before I get really stressed and emotional? Am I being passive-aggressive because I don't feel they help enough? Am I being a martyr? Are they trying to get away with as little as possible? Is this a trait in their family or among their friends? Do they realise how much they are hurting me? Do they know how bad I am feeling? Could they be afraid that it is something serious?

Not enjoying baby and feel guilty about that.

Have I felt like this since the birth? If so, was my birth experience bad? Has the shock of birth affected me? Did I have unrealistic expectations about how I would feel? Did it come on gradually or suddenly? Am I comparing myself and my baby to other people? Do I ever give myself enough time just to sit and cuddle her? Would I feel different about her if I was well rested and the house was tidy? Could I be under so much physical and emotional pressure that I don't have anything much left to feel for her?

Feel very alone.

Am I really alone? Do I have friends or family I could talk to? If so, why aren't I talking to them? Could I talk to a health visitor or a GP? If not, why not? Am I afraid that they will say it is postnatal depression? Do I know anything about PND, or is my fear based on ignorance? Am I afraid they will take my baby away? Do I know who else is out there that I could talk to, like support groups or charities? Might the loneliness be eased by joining supportive baby classes and meeting other mums in similar situations? How important is it that I can talk to and get support from my partner? Did I feel alone before baby arrived?

The reason there are so many questions here is because this is an amalgamation of several cases, so don't be surprised if your case is much simpler.

Some of the questions were focused on baby, and some on you and the adults around you, **because you are just as important as your baby**. Your state of mind and health will have an impact, not only on your ability to make the best decisions for your baby and to care for them, but also on your ability to enjoy the parenting experience.

Don't limit yourself to asking the questions I have suggested here; ask as many different questions as you can think of.

Come at the problem from all directions and try to investigate all angles.

QUESTION YOURSELF THOROUGHLY Ask questions even if you know the answer, because this will enable you to eliminate them from your enquiries. You may know which of your visitors annoy you, or if you can talk to your partner, but sometimes the process of writing them down then crossing them off your list can help focus the direction of your investigation. It can also be a subtle way of drawing your partner's attention to a particular problem; for example, they may not know that it's their mother who makes you stressed, or they may not realise that they themselves appear unapproachable.

They may know they get angry when you are upset, but may not know why, so the more questions you ask the more it will help you to find answers.

There are no right or wrong answers, just *your* answers, and no one is going to see them but you, so please try to be as honest as you possibly can.

Don't play down your feelings or the depth of the problem – remember, this is your chance to take control of your problems and solve them.

BANISH BLAME The only way an answer can be wrong is if it involves blaming either yourself, your partner or your baby. Blame will trigger feelings of anger and guilt, which will cause resentment and will effectively derail your investigation.

If you do feel that something is the fault of your partner, and you feel you can't get past it, then spend some time on your own to consider their behaviour before you talk to them about it.

If you feel they don't help you enough, write that down as your problem, then run through all the questions you can think of regarding what happens, when it happens and how it happens. Ask yourself if their work or personal situation is affecting them. Ask yourself if you are doing anything to cause the problem, make it worse or prevent its resolution.

You may come up with some surprising answers or mitigating circumstances, but even if you get no further forward, the very act of writing it all down will take some of the power out of your anger and will allow you to raise the issue or discuss it in a calmer way.

YOU ARE NOT ALONE If in the process of your investigation you come to the conclusion that something is seriously wrong, don't panic.

There is nothing happening in your life that has not already been experienced by another parent somewhere.

You are not alone. There will be someone who can help you. They may be within the medical profession, part of a volunteer group or charity or a baby care specialist such as myself. There is *always* a way forward!

I have dedicated Chapter 10 to showing you how and where you can get outside help if you feel you need it, but if something is unclear or you are too afraid to ask for help, then please contact me through my website, in confidence, and I will do my best to reassure you and point you in the right direction.

Phase 3: Modification (solution)

In Phase 1, we spent time trying to define the problem and to **assess** what exactly was happening so as to help focus our investigation. In Phase 2, we used record-keeping and **investigation** to uncover the reasons behind the problem, looked for patterns of behaviour and collected data. This will help us move forward into Phase 3, as we find ways to **modify** the situation in order to solve the problem.

GOALS In this phase, you will decide what goals you need to achieve in order to find the solutions to problems, and the more specific you are the better your results will be.

For instance, based on Example A: the feeds are a nightmare, saying that you want the feeds to be better is too vague, and it gives you nothing to work with.

A better suggestion would be to state that you want:

- to feel confident about feeding
- for both you and baby to remain calm and relaxed throughout the feed
- for feeds to last no more than an hour
- to become better at winding
- to eliminate coughing and spluttering

Perhaps you want to adjust your routine so that it's tighter or more fixed, or to be able to have all of the above but be able to apply them to demand-feeding.

Perhaps you want your partner to be able to achieve these same goals.

For Example B: everything is falling apart and I feel useless, the goals might be:

- to stop feeling anxious when leaving the house
- not to feel stressed in the presence of visitors
- to have a flexible routine in place
- to enjoy being a parent
- to improve your health
- for your partner to help you more

The list of things you want to achieve can be as long and as specific as you like, because the first thing you will do is look at your list and prioritise it by deciding what aspect of the situation is causing the most difficulty. Once you have done this, you will need to figure out what has to happen in order for the first goal to be reached.

ARE YOU PREPARED? Taking Example B, you may have decided that having a routine in place will help relieve pressure in many areas, so that is the priority, but now you will have to think about how this can be achieved. What needs to happen to enable you to put the most appropriate routine in place?

To figure this out, we need to go back to our notepads, to a clean page, and run through a mini-investigation by asking ourselves more questions. It will be a little different this time, because you will have already answered the most obvious questions, but now we are looking for less obvious things: what is missing? What do you not know? What skills do you not have? What equipment is missing?

Questions for our mini-investigation might include:

Do I know enough about routines?
What books do I have? Who can I ask? Where can I find reliable information on the internet?

Are there any tools or equipment that can help me (see Chapter 7)?
What do I need? Do I know how to use it? What do I already have? What can I borrow? Where can I buy what I need quickly?

What routine will suit both baby and myself/my partner/family/ lifestyle?
When would I like to start and end the day? What time does my partner go to and come home from work? When do I have to leave for work? When do my other children have to go to nursery/school/ activities?

DON'T GET BOGGED DOWN IN DETAIL If the questions you ask raise even more questions, don't get confused or bogged down with it all. Subdivide the question, start another page and focus on one small part at a time. For instance, you may need a separate page for each of the above questions, and it may feel too complicated, but don't get stressed – just work on one question at a time and stay focused.

At times you may feel that there is so much you don't know, and wonder how you will ever figure it all out, but I promise you: all new parents feel the same way. You will get there if you take it one little bit at a time . . . baby steps!

The next step after this fact-finding stage is to decide on a **plan of action**.

HOW TO MOVE FORWARD What can you do to change the situation, fix the problem, solve the case?

This is where you get creative and inventive, where you apply your knowledge of your situation and come up with something, anything, that might make a difference.

You may decide to implement big changes, such as changes to your parenting style or your feeding method. You may seek medical or expert help, and completely rearrange your daily schedule or swap parenting roles with your partner. Other changes may be much smaller, such as where you sit to feed baby, or what position you hold them in, how you wind them, what bottles or teats you use. You might choose to add equipment such as pacifiers and swaddles, use music or white noise, or limit or eliminate their use.

This might look incredibly complicated as you read through all the possible problems. But after studying the results of your investigation, you might realise that all that is needed is for baby to have a longer sleep before feeds, or that your partner needs to pick up supper on the way home from work and cook it, to give you a much-needed break so that you have the strength for the night feeds.

That is why this process works so well, because often by the time you have worked your way through it to this point, you already know what it is you need to do, and will wonder why you didn't see it before.

THERE IS NO RIGHT OR WRONG In your search for possible modifications, it is tempting to try to concentrate on finding the 'right' answer, but remember: there is no right answer. Anything you come up with is worthy of consideration, and sometimes it helps just to throw out suggestions, no matter how random they seem, in a rapid brainstorming session until you have a nice big list you can then sift through.

What you are creating is a plan of action that is designed by you for your particular situation for your family and your baby, and which will, therefore, be much more relevant than any one-size-fits-all solution written by someone who has never met you or your family.

Remind yourself that you probably won't get it perfect first time, so for whatever plan you devise, be prepared to implement it, test it for twenty-four hours, record the results and then modify any aspect of it that is not quite right.

I have found that the morning is the best time to try anything new, as it is the perfect time to 'reset' things.

Decide what equipment you will need and assemble it the night before, including notebooks, diaries, and so on.

> A useful tool is a Dictaphone or voice recorder app on your phone, so note-making is easy and hands-free.

Have everything you intend to do written down clearly, step by step, as it will help you feel confident and in control and will act as a reminder if you get confused. A written plan is also vital if there is more than one person caring for the baby, so everyone concerned is doing exactly the same thing at the same time, otherwise much of your hard work may be undone in an instant.

Some plans are easier to implement than others, such as those which involve just the immediate members of the household. Those that include extended family or friends, or even health specialists, can require more preparation.

In Example B: everything is falling apart and I feel useless, above, it may be the case that relatives need to be informed of new 'house rules', such as visits are by invitation only and are for a set length of time. This might be difficult for some people to understand, but they will accept it more easily if it is for a set period, e.g. two weeks, 'while things settle down', or 'to let the parent get a bit of rest'.

If a visit to a doctor or a talk with the health visitor is necessary, get this done as a matter of priority, as this will give you hard facts you can act upon. It will also help rule out some factors, which may help focus your investigation further and can often alleviate a lot of fears.

For the anxious parent in Example B, the plan could look something like this:

1. Schedule appointment at doctor's regarding general health check and heavy bleeding, and raise question of postnatal depression.

2. Ban all visitors for one week, then implement invitation-only visits lasting no more than one hour, based around baby's feed times.

3. Partner to have quiet word with his mother whose 'helpful comments' are upsetting.

4. Set routine in place that starts the day at 7 a.m. and includes three-hourly feeds until the last feed of the day at 10 p.m.

5. Wake baby for feeds and encourage her to sleep for at least an hour before each feed so she is well rested and won't keep falling asleep, making the feeds too long.

6. Make each feed a bit more 'businesslike', taking no more than an hour, with baby being winded frequently and nappy-changed halfway through to wake her up.

7. Bath time is too stressful, so drop for two weeks to give parents time to recover and adapt.

8. Parents' roles: the parent who is staying at home with baby should be given time to adjust to the new routine without having to worry about anything else. To this end, all shopping for the week to be done beforehand, consisting of healthy food to be cooked by the stay-at-home parent Monday to Thursday. On Friday, order a takeaway. Food to be cooked over the weekend by the parent who has worked during the week, and this parent will also help with chores and laundry to stop it building up.

9. During the weekend, both parents to take time to relax with their baby either at home or on a gentle walk, just to be a family together.

10. Every day, both parents to help to keep detailed records of how they and their baby are reacting to the changes, taking time to review each day before bedtime and make any necessary adjustments.

11. At the end of the week, both parents to review the week and discuss the results, making any necessary adjustments.

12. If all is going to plan, the anxious parent will use the stability of the new routine as a basis for calm, unhurried preparation for a trip out to visit supportive friends.

13. Relatives/friends to be invited for a one-hour visit, but only one set at a time and only every other day to give the anxious parent time to recover.

For Example A: the feeds are a nightmare, a plan could look something like this:

1. Tighten up routine so that the day starts at 7.30 a.m. and the last feed at 10.30 p.m., and feed strictly at three-hourly intervals through the day so baby never gets overly hungry.

2. Make sure baby is asleep in his moses basket at least one and a half hours before each feed, so he doesn't get overtired.

3. Try the extra-slow-flow bottle, but also have usual bottle ready and on hand in case he hates the slow bottle.

4. Make sure everything needed for the feed is set up at least half an hour before it is due, to prevent him getting impatient and worked up if he wakes early and to prevent parent feeling rushed. This includes drinks/snack for the parent, television remotes, notebook, muslin cloths, nappy-changing basket, bottles, swaddle, and so on.

5. Have favourite TV box set ready and start watching *before* the feed, once everything is set up, to distract yourself and avoid the stress produced by anticipation of the feed.

6. If baby coughs and splutters early on in feed, just comfort him briefly and resume feed as soon as possible rather than try to wind him, so he doesn't have the chance to get wound up.

7. Feed him until he stops naturally, then give him a good winding for at least ten minutes to see how much more wind he may be holding.

8. Change the nappy in the middle of the feed in case it helps dislodge more wind.

9. Aim for the feed to last no more than an hour.

10. When he has finished feeding, wind him for a minimum of fifteen minutes, using passive methods if he falls asleep so he doesn't keep waking up when put down in his moses basket.

11. After doing this for forty-eight hours and recording the results, assess the routine and feeds and see if anything needs adjusting.

12. If he is still waking with wind, try swaddling him for all his sleeps for twenty-four hours and assess results.

13. If still waking with wind, try using Infacol (simethicone) before feeds for twenty-four hours, and again, assess results.

You will note that in the last two points of Example A, the parents are only changing one thing at a time, then assessing each step before making further changes. This is because if you change everything at the same time, you will not know what it is that is making the difference, so may be giving the Infacol or swaddling unnecessarily. Though neither of these solutions are harmful in any way, there is no point spending money and time on something if you don't need to.

Remember, this is an investigation, so you need to be aware of the effect of everything that is going on and the impact of every change you make, so take it one step at a time.

NOTE I am not suggesting you should start your day at 7 a.m., or feed baby every three hours. Every baby and each situation will be different.

When you first read this chapter, you may find it a little overwhelming, but the three AIM stages are designed simply to help you identify the problem, understand why it is happening and find a solution.

5.

Planning ahead

The same process of Assess, Investigate and Modify also applies to preparing for known future events, and can be used to great effect when planning big occasions such as holidays, or minor ones such as a doctor's appointment or a lunch date.

The good news is that hopefully, at this point, you will have already used this process to eliminate existing problems, so you will be starting from a position of strength, already knowing yourselves as parents and your baby's needs and preferences, which should make things a lot easier.

Remember that the most important considerations are your baby's needs for being

- well fed
- well rested
- comfortable

For your baby to be comfortable, you need to ensure that they are thoroughly winded and as calm and relaxed as possible, so please bear in mind the potential environmental stresses of temperature, light, noise and handling/over-handling that they are likely to encounter.

ASSESSMENT PHASE The first thing you will be doing is thinking about the planned situation and gathering as much information as you can. The more detailed your plan, the better your solutions will be.

Basically what you are trying to imagine is what exactly is going to happen and how the event may alter yours and baby's environment, i.e. how your normal day-to-day life will change.

INVESTIGATION PHASE In this next step, you will investigate the projected situation to try to predict how these changes will affect your baby based on what you already know about their temperament, their reactions and their biological needs, not forgetting to consider your own reactions and needs as well as those of the rest of your immediate family.

MODIFICATION PHASE By this stage, you will have a list of potential problems for which you can then create a list of possible solutions, and will make sure you have all the equipment you may need, enough time for travel and alternative plans in place as backup in order to survive, enjoy and recover from your event.

I have chosen five events which require, or would benefit from, careful planning, and will talk you through each one to give you some idea of what might be involved in preparing for it.

Some of what I suggest may seem obvious to more experienced parents, but I am being as thorough as I can to provide as much help as possible for new, inexperienced or anxious/exhausted parents. Please note that carers, grandparents, family and friends can also use this process either in helping the new parents plan an event, or in planning their own event where young babies will be present.

Asking yourself so many questions can result in a lot of details to process mentally, so I find making lists helpful. If you do all your planning in the same notebook, you will create a useful resource to help with future planning.

A family gathering at home

This may be a group of relatives or friends coming to see the baby, for a sibling's birthday or for any other reason.

You already know how your life runs normally, so how might that change?

How many people are coming? Adults or children?

Who is the focus? Baby, a sibling, parent, relative or friend?

What time are they arriving? Might some people arrive early? How long are they staying? Might some stay later?

Will you have to prepare/serve food? Who is helping you? How long will preparation take? When will you have to start?

Some people may find this amount of detail unnecessary, but the more tired and anxious you are, or the more difficult your baby is, then the more important it is for you to have clear and accurate information, because knowing exactly what is happening and when will be a huge confidence boost.

This initial round of fact-gathering will enable you to begin investigating and considering how you and your baby will be affected; for instance, how sensitive baby is to environmental factors.

You might find it helpful at this point to write a brief list of your baby's temperament and character traits as a reminder of what to look for.

- How will baby react to the increased noise level, especially if there are going to be other children around?

- How will they cope with being handled by different people? Can they sleep through it all?

- Do they usually need peace and quiet for a calm feed?

- How will you cope with having to feed and wind baby in front of people? Are you confident or anxious if others hold your baby? How will you feel if they start offering 'helpful advice'?

- Some more robust babies and parents just sail through all this with no problems, but more often than not there will be complications at some point in proceedings. This is usually in reaction to disturbed feed and sleep and over-handling, so you need to come up with modifications that will allow you to protect your baby at these times.

- Would it help to alter the baby's routine so that they get a good feed and a good sleep before anyone arrives? If so, how will you do this? Will you start the day early, or later to adjust feed times?

Morning is always a good time to make any changes to routine, even if the one feed you are aiming to change is in the afternoon or evening, as it makes change gradual rather than sudden.

- If timings are difficult, could you use a snack feed or split feed to make the adaptation work?

- If you think baby would benefit from an extra-long sleep before the event, how could you achieve this? Make the previous sleep shorter? Give baby extra food? Take them out for a walk in the fresh air? Put them to sleep in a darkened room, even if you don't normally do this?

Baths can help to tire a baby and relax them, and can be used at any time of day to help prepare them for sleep – you don't have to keep them just for evenings.

- During the event, will you stay in the room with your guests to feed and wind baby? If your baby is tricky to feed or wind, will you be able to concentrate sufficiently with all the distractions? Will you be able to refuse politely if your guests ask to 'have a go' at feeding, or offer to wind? If you don't feel confident enough to do this, can you prime your partner or an accomplice to help explain that it is not a good idea?

- Do you have somewhere you can retreat to if you want to feed baby in private? If so, how will you make it clear to 'helpful' guests that you'd prefer to be alone (if that is your wish)? Can you set this retreat up with everything you might possibly need for the feed, including spares of everything to make it as smooth and easy as possible? Will there be food and drink for you? Will your partner know that when you are feeding they are on duty as the host so no one need disturb you?

- If your baby is going to protest about being passed around, is there anything you can do to make it more bearable for them? Would a pacifier help? Or a swaddle?

- If baby was swaddled firmly or wrapped in a blanket, would it help you feel more confident about other people holding them? Would it help if you or someone you trusted was the one to carry baby around from person to person? Do you (or does your partner) know your baby well enough to spot the early signs of impending meltdown so that you can rescue them before they get too upset?

- If baby is starting to get stressed, do you know how to calm and soothe them? Can you do it in company, or will you need to go somewhere quiet? Where will you go? Can you prepare the things you might need, such as music, pacifiers, swaddle, toys for distraction?

If baby is being passed around and handled by other people, you might find it useful to attach pacifiers and favourite comforters to baby's clothing using a pacifier clip.

This will prevent items being lost or dropped on the floor and given back to baby without being cleaned or replaced.

- When baby needs to sleep, do you know how to spot the signs? Are you going to keep them in the same room as everyone else? Will they be swaddled, cuddled or put down in a basket or pram? If so, will they be safe from rampaging older children or curious younger ones? Might you get them off to sleep in a different room, then bring them back in once asleep? Would it be better if they slept in their own room?

If you have a partner or someone helping you, it is important that you prepare a plan together so you both know what is likely to happen and what plans need to be in place in order to cope, not just with baby's needs but with your own and each other's.

It may be that the stronger or calmer parent can be responsible for suggesting that the anxious parent takes baby out for a feed or for some peace and quiet. They can do this even if the baby is fine, if they notice that their partner is looking stressed and could do with a break . . . babies can be a great excuse for time out!

Sometimes the hardest part of a family gathering is not the baby, but the personalities and politics of the people involved. There will usually be a mix of loud or opinionated people (some meaning well but others less so) and quiet and calm people, those who are easy-going alongside those who are easily offended. There can be undercurrents of competition and favouritism and good and bad humours, all in one room, topped off with excitement and expectations about meeting the new baby or cele-brating an occasion.

This can all be easy to cope with under normal circumstances, but can be much harder to cope with if you have a new baby when you are much more likely to be tired, stressed, disorganised and often overwhelmed, so it is worth spending time thinking about how certain family members may be calmed down or en-couraged, and how best to make sure everyone feels included and accommodated, e.g. making sure that both mothers-in-law get equal baby-holding time, that siblings or visiting children don't get ignored (which can lead to their own meltdowns), or that overbearing relatives don't hog the baby.

Quiet words could be had beforehand either warning some people to behave, or priming others to be on hand to help.

> It can be very useful to have a secret code to use so part-ners or family members can signal to each other if some-thing requires action.

There is also nothing wrong with letting any routine go and making it up as you go along, as long as baby doesn't get too upset. In this case, make sure you have a plan in place to help you get baby back into their routine once guests have left. Quite often a nice full tummy helps baby settle, so, using the same process, you can ask yourself how do I calm them down enough to get a really good feed? How do I get them back on track if we are half an hour/an hour/two hours off schedule? If they have slept a lot, how can I keep them awake for a while to get them tired? Would a bath help? Would a split feed help?

There will always be unexpected occurrences, such as the time a client's family arrived to see baby and celebrate a birthday. All went well apart from someone setting out party poppers on the table when the parents and I were busy elsewhere, so that when the meal started, the baby, who was fast asleep in the pram in the same room, was woken by twenty-three party poppers! She screamed in terror and it took well over half an hour to calm the poor little girl down, but even things like this become much less of a disaster if you know how to calm your baby and have a quiet room set up with everything you might need.

A good, sound, well-thought-out plan will result in you, your baby and everyone else being able to enjoy the event with a calm and happy baby who can be cuddled and passed around while you relax, knowing that you have planned for every possible eventuality and that you have a safe, fully equipped place you can retreat to when needed.

A medical appointment or treatment

In your assessment, you need to make sure you know the time of the appointment, the likelihood and length of delays, the location, time needed for travel, the best route, mode of transport, cost of transport, location and cost of parking and to make sure you have money and contact details in case you get lost or delayed, and have a fully charged phone.

Travelling anywhere with a baby can be stressful at times, so knowing all the details in advance can make it much more likely you will get there on time. If you are delayed, the fact that you can call and let the doctor or hospital know can take some of the pressure off you.

Now you know where you have to be and at what time, you can start thinking about how you can prepare your baby so that they will stay as well rested, well fed and comfortable for as long as possible.

- What time do you need to feed baby before you leave to allow for thorough winding?

If you baby still has wind, putting them on their back in a pram or in a car seat (where they are folded in the middle) can make them very uncomfortable and is likely to lead to crying or screaming, so make sure you leave plenty of time for winding.

- How can you adjust the feeding times? Give a snack feed, split feed, extra feed? Start the day early? If the appointment is something like an injection or an examination, might you be better timing feeds so that you can give the baby breast or bottle as a comfort straight after the procedure?

- Should you make sure they have a good sleep beforehand or try to get them to sleep en route?

- How is your baby likely to react? What are their patience levels? What is their tolerance for pain? What will you need to help calm or distract them? What equipment will you need (swaddle, pacifier, sling, toys for comfort, toys for distraction, medicine, bottles, formula, breastfeeding supplies such as pads, cover-up, nipple cream, water to drink, pump for expressing plus spare storage bottles)?

- How will *you* react? How will you cope if your baby screams or has to be held down by medical staff?

Swaddling your baby fully or partially can make them a lot easier to hold for examinations or procedures that won't be obstructed by the fabric.

- Can you cope with needles and blood? I had one client who fainted at the sight of blood, so we planned medical appointments very carefully and she stayed outside the room, though we had to think on our feet when her son stood on a carpet gripper and bled profusely. Luckily we had two sofas, one for her and one for her son!

- If you are unsure how you will react, can you take someone with you to help?

- If the procedure will take a long time, do you know exactly what you might need for four hours, eight hours, overnight or a couple of days? Who can you ask to bring you things you might need or to care for baby while you have a break?

- If you are a single parent or have no one to help, how will you cope if your baby is in hospital? When would be the best time for you to leave your baby to go home and collect things or take a break? Would night time be better, because less traffic means shorter travel times? Are there places locally where you can take a walk or buy supplies?

- If breastfeeding, are you happy to feed in public or will you need a room for privacy? If so, can you arrange feed times to coincide with the availability of a separate room, such as at the doctor's surgery, arriving early to feed or staying afterwards?

Doctors' surgeries and hospitals are very used to women asking for privacy for feeding, so never feel nervous about requesting it. It is your right to feed your baby!

- If your baby is having a longer medical procedure or surgery, will there be somewhere near the waiting area where you can feed? Can you phone and check in advance to help with your planning?

- Are you ready for any aftercare that might be needed after a vaccination? Do you have a thermometer? Do you know how to use it? Would it boost your confidence levels to practise beforehand so you know you can get a consistent reading? Do you have liquid paracetamol and ibuprofen in case it is needed? Do you know the recommended dose for your baby's age?

- Can you give medicine without spilling it? Would it help you to practise beforehand using milk or water in a syringe?

Swaddling your baby and using a medicine syringe makes it much easier and more likely that you will be able to give a full and accurate dose.

- If baby is ill, do you have a diary or record of their illness or behaviour to show the doctor in case you are too stressed or focused on baby to remember accurately? If you haven't kept a record, can you remember anything now, while you are relaxed at home, that you can jot down?

If you are worried about a cough or some other symptom that might not be present during the actual medical appointment, it is always useful to take a video to show the doctor.

- Can you make provision for the care of your other children in case you are delayed?

- Are you confident you can readjust the routine once you are home again? Do you have everything you need to care for baby for two or three days after the procedure, so you don't have to cope with the stress of having to take a sick or miserable baby out shopping?

- Do you have contact details for the health visitor, midwife, doctor or hospital and out-of-hours medical helplines in case you have any concerns?

Once you have run through everything in your mind, assessing and investigating every potential problem, and have put plans in place to cope with them, it is worth taking the time to prepare everything you physically need the day before, if possible.

Pack baby's bag and make sure you have plenty of spare nappies, wipes, clothes, and so on, plus any feeds, toys, distractions and comforters you will need, along with your red book if you have one (in the UK this acts as a record of all medical procedures done and when, including vaccinations).

> Pack items separately in clear plastic wallets or make-up bags so you can see exactly what is in them and can access them more easily in a hurry.

Getting ready the night before gives you the chance to recheck the next morning and make sure you have remembered everything. If you are changing baby's routine, things might get confusing and unpredictable, making it less likely you will have a chance for a last-minute check.

It also gives you one less thing to be stressed about if you are anxious, and the calmer you can be, the calmer your baby will be.

As a new parent, taking your baby for any medical procedure, no matter how minor, can be extremely stressful, so the more planning you can do, the more confident you will be, which in turn will be reassuring for your baby.

The more experienced parents will have learnt the importance of all the checks and the planning through their mistakes – as have I. My intention in going through it in such detail is to bring the benefit of experience to inexperienced parents, enabling them to become competent and confident much earlier on in their parenting journey.

Furthermore, this problem-solving and planning process has the added benefit in that the more you do it, the more it will become a habit. It becomes second nature to assess situations and look for potential problems and solutions, to the point where it kicks in automatically in emergency situations.

I was with a client whose baby stopped breathing, so, in a state of shock, we had a midnight ambulance trip followed by a two-week hospital stay. She was a single mother whose family were in the US, so it was just the two of us, but we took our knowledge of the baby, ourselves and his routine and used it to formulate very quickly a plan of action and a method of surviving which involved me caring for him at night while mum did the days.

Every shift change, we worked out what would happen over the next twelve hours and made sure one of us could bring in anything we needed for baby and for ourselves. We already had a diary of his normal routine and behaviour, which proved very useful to the medical staff, and we kept a detailed record of everything that happened in hospital so we both knew what was going on and how baby was reacting, even if one of us was absent at the time.

After he recovered and was discharged, we continued the record-keeping and used the **AIM** process to help both ourselves and baby readjust to life at home, coping with his medical care and routine and follow-up appointments and with our exhaustion, fears and emotional reactions to the experience. After three days we were all well rested, well fed and as comfortable and calm as you could possibly expect, because we had thought our way through every single aspect of the situation, imagined every possible scenario and were confident that we could cope.

A social event away from home

It is uncanny the number of weddings, christenings and important anniversaries that seem to crop up once you have a new baby, and for inexperienced parents this can seem quite a daunting prospect.

Quite often I listen to parents arguing back and forth about whether or not they should go, how they can get out of it and whether or not they will be easily forgiven if they cancel. When asked for my opinion, we do some fact-finding and have a discussion such as the one I will talk you through here. Then, unless the situation is extremely difficult, I am usually able to reassure them that, with careful planning, attending the occasion should be fine.

The process is the same as planning for an event at your own home, with many of the same considerations, the difference being that at a venue away from home, much of what happens is beyond your control. This can make things more 'interesting', but it means you have to be more thorough in your planning and prepared to be more creative in your solutions.

You need to know the usual facts, such as where the venue is, how you will get there, what time you need to leave the house and how much time you should allow for delays, but you also need to ascertain when you are expected to arrive and what time the actual event starts, as these can be different.

You will also need to find out as much as you can about the facilities and how the event will proceed, so contact the venue and ask the event organisers, family and friends.

When contacting venues, it is always useful to explain why you are asking certain questions. If they know you have a baby, they may volunteer information or make their own suggestions as to how things could be organised or made easier.

- You will have a lot of baby paraphernalia. Is the car park close to the venue? Is it easy to get a taxi from the station, or should you book one in advance?

- Is any part of the event outdoors or is it all indoors? Is there heating? Is it likely to be too hot or too cold? How many people are going? Will there be music, and of what sort? For baby's ears there is a big difference between background piano music and a live rock band! Will there be many other children? What ages (even the best-behaved children can get overtired, overexcited and very loud sometimes, which needs to be taken into account if you have a noise-sensitive baby)?

- Is there any time, for instance during a wedding or christening, when you will need your baby to be quiet? If so, when is this likely to be and at which point in the ceremony? How will you cope with a crying baby? Is a pacifier likely to be enough, or should you try to sit near the doors for a quick exit?

- Is it a sit-down meal or a buffet? What time is that? How long is it likely to last? If baby is sleeping is there room near your table for your pram/buggy, or will you have to leave baby a short distance away? If so, how will you cope with that? How will you cope if baby is awake during a meal? Can you eat one-handed, with them on your lap (an acquired skill!), or do you have someone who can share baby duties while you take it in turns to eat? If you need to leave the table during the meal to feed or settle your baby, will someone be able to bring you some food?

Always make sure you have some snacks/drink in the baby bag in case you get stranded somewhere dealing with baby and miss your meal. You are much more likely to be able to cope with a difficult baby if you aren't too hungry yourself.

- If both parents normally like a drink, who will be the designated sober person to care for the baby and to drive? If you are a breastfeeding mother who wants a drink, do you know the safe limits or have enough expressed milk ready? Is there some way of warming baby's milk if needed?

- If you are allowing family or friends to feed baby, do they know how baby likes to be fed? Can they wind properly, and settle baby to sleep?

People are much more likely to follow instructions regarding baby's feeds and general routine if they are written down, so it is worth taking the time to make a simple guide to keep in baby's changing bag.

- Will there be a room available to feed your baby or have some quiet time, or will you need to use your car or go for a walk?

- How will your baby react to noise and activity when they need to sleep? Is there somewhere quiet for them to sleep? If not, will they sleep in their pram if you take them for a walk? If so, will they stay asleep if you stop walking, or will you need to keep walking to keep them asleep? What will you do if the weather is bad? Is there somewhere nearby that is safe and suitable for walks?

- How will your baby react to being handled by strangers? Will there be a lot of people wanting to hold baby? Will they be the sort of people you will want holding your baby?

> If you are worried or feel that things might get stressful for you or baby, it might be better to have a 'no hold' policy, explaining that your baby gets upset if held by strangers. This can give you the advantage of being able to accept help from close family or friends without offending others.

- What time will the event end? Do you want to set a definite departure time, or leave it fluid in case you are having a great time and baby is fine?

- Are you returning home the same day? How long will the return journey take? Will you be planning to feed and wind baby before you leave, or feed on the train or in a service station? If so, does whoever is driving realise that a good feed and wind may take an hour or more?

- If you are staying overnight, what will you need for baby? Where will they sleep? What equipment will you need?

Always take more than you need in case of accidents or unforeseen events, or to lend to less well-prepared parents!

- Will you need blackout blinds, music or white noise?

- Once you get home, how do you plan to get baby back into their normal routine? Even if you normally have no routine, how will you best be able to get some rest if you or your partner are exhausted or a little hung-over?

- Can you plan the day after the event as a quiet day, in order to allow baby time to recover if they have got off schedule or overtired?

This list might seem exhaustive (and exhausting), but remember, I am trying to cover every eventuality, so many of these questions or potential problems might not be applicable to your occasion.

It is sometimes the case that when working with clients, most of my careful planning goes completely out of the window, baby is taken all day by a very capable relative and I am redundant and told to go off and enjoy myself, which I do (usually managing to keep one eye on baby). The routine is ignored, yet somehow baby gets enough milk and sleep to stay happy, but even this is planned for. I know we have enough of everything we need for every eventuality, so I can relax. I know I have plans in my head for coping if things go wrong, and I am confident that I know baby well enough to be able to reinstate a semblance of a routine at the drop of a hat either at the event, back at home, or the next day – all because of this sort of mental preparation.

It is very useful to try to plan the day after the event as a quiet, stay-at-home day to give you and baby time to recover and get yourselves back into your routine.

The fact that you have worked through the process and planned thoroughly will give you, even as a very new parent, the confidence you need to attempt these kinds of social occasions, allowing you to share special events with your family and friends and experience them as a family, with your baby.

A foreign holiday

While most of us have travelled abroad at some point and know what it entails, once you have a baby you will find that travelling overseas can become much more complicated and requires a lot of planning and preparation.

The first two considerations are the baby's passport and vaccinations, both of which may need several weeks' notice depending on where you are going, so should not be left until the last minute.

Passports used to be available for babies and children on a same-day basis, but to prevent parental child abduction this is no longer the case in the UK. Apply as soon as you can – don't leave it until the last minute!

Travel to 'first world' countries is very safe, and as long as you are careful about any water that is used to wash baby or make feeds, there is little to worry about, unless you are in an area where malaria is present, in which case you need to use mosquito nets around baby as they may be too young to take malaria medication, so check with a paediatrician or specialist travel centre.

Travel to developing countries can require a little more careful thought. Some of these countries may still have illnesses present that have been eliminated from our own country, or pose little threat here, such as polio, whooping cough and diphtheria, so please raise the question of vaccination with your health visitor, GP or with the Health Protection Agency or a specialised travel clinic if your baby is too young to have been fully vaccinated. Other vaccines may be needed for specific destinations, so again, check with healthcare professionals.

If you decide against vaccinations that are advised for your destination, check that your baby is still covered by your travel insurance in case anything happens and you need medical support.

You will need to check the obvious information such as flight and check-in times, method and duration of transport to airport or train station, length of flight and time difference, along with duration of any stopovers and hotel transfers, as all these will impact baby's routine.

You will also need to know what baby items you can buy at your destination such as formula, nappies, baby food, bottled water (only certain brands are suitable for babies). If you plan to buy things there, at least make sure you have enough with you in baby's cabin bag for forty-eight hours to take pressure off yourselves having to shop straight away, and in case the hold luggage goes astray.

Also consider how you will transport your baby once at your destination. Many taxi/transfer companies offer what they term 'child seats', but in my experience, these are often only suitable for older children and are useless for newborns. Many people find it easier to travel with their own car seat and check it in with the hold luggage.

Please familiarise yourself with the rules about taking liquids through security, as anything over 100ml will be confiscated unless it is baby milk. This is usually checked or scanned, but sometimes you are asked to drink a little from some or all of the bottles, in front of security staff, which on one occasion led to my having to drink someone else's breastmilk! I now take powdered formula, or check with the airport pharmacies as to whether we can buy ready-made formula in Customs, along with any bottled water we need.

If taking breastmilk, be prepared to taste it if required but don't pack the milk with sealed cool packs containing liquid as they cannot be tested and so will be confiscated, leaving you as I was left on one occasion, having to beg for ice from a champagne and seafood bar once you're through security!

You can also buy bottles of infant paracetamol and ibuprofen through Customs but I also always take individual sachets as they are much lighter and less prone to breaking and swamping everything else in the bag with sticky mess.

Wet wipes are amazingly versatile, so take plenty as you will use them a lot. My favourites are Water Wipes – they're just water and fruit extract, so can safely be used on baby's face (as well as your own), for wiping bottles, pacifiers or toys that fall on the floor, cleaning up sick from seats and carpets.

For young babies, airlines offer skycots, which are bassinets that can be strapped safely onto a fold-out shelf attached to the seats in front of the bulkheads (the airplane's compartment dividers). They can be very useful as you can put baby down to sleep or play while you eat, but there are usually only one or two per bulkhead, in the centre of the plane, so availability is limited. Some airlines allow you to book them, but others allocate them on the day, or give priority to the youngest babies, so check with your airline in advance.

A very common question about long-haul flights is whether it is best to fly during the day or overnight, and having done this many times my preference is always for *daytime* flights. Although the vibration and noise of the plane's engines can have a soporific effect and help babies sleep, they do not always sleep reliably or consistently, so it is unlikely they will sleep for long stretches during a night flight.

Also there are so many things that can disrupt their sleep, such as people wanting to get past you to go to the bathroom, seat belt signs going on and meals and snacks being served, which can all add up to a very unsettled and upset baby. This is bad enough to deal with in the daytime, but trying to manage a screaming baby when other passengers are trying to sleep can be a nightmare, so I find it less stressful for everyone to get a daytime flight where possible.

There is so much to consider that the best way to keep it manageable is to run through the holiday in your head and work through things in the same order they will occur, starting at the beginning:

- How will you adjust baby's routine so that they are not due a feed either on the journey to the airport or while you are checking in? Will you start the day earlier or later, give a snack feed or split feed?

> Feeds at airports tend to take longer than feeds at home because of the many distractions for baby, so always allow yourselves extra time to finish the feed and for adequate winding – dealing with a windy baby on take-off is no fun!

- Are you aware of the luggage allowance for a baby? Most airlines allow a suitcase plus an on-board bag but always check.

- Once you have checked your car seat in, how will you transport baby? Are you taking your buggy/pram? Most airlines allow you to take your buggy/pram right up to the gate before checking them in, but always confirm beforehand. Are you using a sling/baby carrier?

- When is baby's next feed due? Will you do it once you have checked in, or when you have gone through security?

- Airports are massively stimulating environments with lots of noise, activity and light. How will your baby react? If they are sensitive, might they find it more comforting to be carried in a sling, facing inward, and maybe with the top of the carrier covered by a muslin (thin and breathable) to shut out some of the stimulation? If they are not so sensitive, might they be better facing outward in a sling (if old enough) or in a pram/buggy so they can see and be distracted?

> If you don't have time to wind your baby properly before needing to move around the airport, put them in a sling as the upright position is more comfortable than sitting, and can also help wind bubbles come up as you move.

- What is the best way to comfort your baby if they get upset? Make sure you pack lots of spare pacifiers, toys, teethers, and so on in baby's cabin bag so you never run out.

- If you have an aisle seat with baby on your lap, be very vigilant as there is a danger the flight attendants might accidentally spill drinks from trays over baby as they go up and down the aisle. Having experienced this myself, I now usually ask to swap seats.

- If travelling with siblings, will you have enough toys, snacks, iPads, games, books, and so on to occupy them?

- Once landed and through passport control, how long will it take to transfer to the hotel/accommodation? When would be the best time to feed baby?

- Once at your hotel/accommodation, will you have everything you need to feed or settle baby to sleep with you, or will you have to request anything such as kettles or cots?

- Do you have a plan for settling baby into the new time zone? If you arrive at your destination in daytime but baby's night time, how will you keep baby awake until bedtime? Would it be best to allow a fairly long sleep but follow that by short naps to get them through, or just have short but more frequent naps? What else might distract baby and keep them awake for some of the time? Might they enjoy a walk? Will it be cool enough? Could you walk anywhere indoors with air conditioning, such as shopping malls or hotel lobbies?

> When travelling, it is useful to take baby's diary or notebook and continue making notes to help investigate and modify any problems as you go.

- What might be the earliest you could put baby down and have them sleep for as long as possible?

- If you do put baby down to sleep early, how will you eat? Is there room service? Are there shops nearby? Could one parent go and get food while baby sleeps? If you have siblings with you, how will you keep them occupied and fed?

- How will you cope if baby is awake a lot during the night? If there are two parents, will you take it in turns, or will it be the responsibility of just one parent? If you have siblings, have you made plans for adjusting and altering their sleep patterns?

- What will you need to help give baby clear sleep signals? Will you need to take music/white noise gadgets? Will baby need swaddles or comforters? Will they need blackout blinds?

Tinfoil or black bin bags make excellent emergency blackout blinds as they are easily procured and cut to size and can be stuck to the window using any sticky liquid such as cooking oil, moisturiser, sunscreen, even nappy cream, which can then be cleaned with a cloth or wet wipe before you leave.

- How will your baby cope with the temperature if it is very different from what they are used to? Will they be outside much? Sunscreen is not suitable for babies under six months, so what will you need to protect them? Sun hat with brim or neck cover? Long-sleeved clothing?

Sunshade/beach umbrella? Will you need to arrange your day so that you can stay inside during the hottest periods – usually between 10 a.m. and 2 p.m.? How will this work if you have older children? Are there attractions you can visit with air conditioning if you need to stay out of the sun?

- How will you feed when you are out and about? What are local opinions on breastfeeding in public? Can you feed at restaurants, or are there dedicated feeding rooms? Might these be women-only? If so, can the woman cope on her own? Will the other parent be able to cope with any other children on their own? If not, how can you plan trips out around baby's feeds so that everyone's needs are met and you all enjoy yourselves?

- Do you know where the nearest doctor or hospital is to your accommodation, in case of emergency?

Always give some thought to planning the trip home at least two days before you return in order to give yourself time to adjust the routine, or buy necessary supplies and avoid a last-minute stressful rush.

- What time will it be when you land back home? Bearing in mind you will all be exhausted, would it be a good idea to feed baby on the plane so you can concentrate on getting home as quickly as possible?

- Do you have a plan for getting baby back into your usual
  time zone when you get back? Will you try to do it
  gradually or all at once? Are you confident you can cope
  with however baby is reacting, and are just going to play it
  by ear?

This list of things to consider may seem overwhelming at first, but you will find that as you face and answer all the questions, you will feel more confident and in control. Start planning well in advance of your departure, make lists of information and equipment and pack at least two days before you leave so that you have time to buy anything you realise you are missing.

Think carefully about what you really need to take so you don't overpack. Hotels provide spare blankets and towels, which you can use to soften hard cot mattresses, as blankets or play mats or to make a temporary sleepyhead-type mattress (a mattress with raised padded edges that cocoon your baby) if that is what you use at home.

Muslins pack very flat, are easily washed and dried and can double up as swaddles, changing mats, towels, sunshades, flannels and play mats.

Babies love looking around them at new things, and will be happy to play with anything you can find in the hotel room or apartment, so you don't need to take many toys, just a few small favourites.

To save room, you can buy travel packs of cold water-sterilising tablets in a special heavy-duty plastic bag, which work wonderfully, and mean you can leave the bulky steriliser at home. If you are staying in a house or apartment, boil bottles for ten minutes to sterilise them.

Think carefully about what you will need on the plane and for the first forty-eight hours, and make sure that it goes on the plane with you and not in the hold, so you never find yourself missing something important.

Think of every way in which you can make life as easy and simple as possible and you will have a wonderful time, and if anything does go wrong, you know exactly how to work through the problem: just sit down with your notebook and remember to **Assess**, **Investigate** and **Modify**.

I have travelled with many families, and the flight is always feared the most, but careful planning can eliminate the majority of the problems you are likely to encounter and airline staff are usually very friendly and helpful. Some airlines even have dedicated 'sky nannies' whose job it is to help any parents, so please don't be put off travelling. Your first holiday as a family can be a wonderful experience (don't forget your passports!).

Baby's development

You can also use the **AIM** process to cope with upcoming changes as your baby develops. It works in exactly the same way as it does for problem-solving and planning special events.

Through using this process, you will by now have got to know your baby and yourselves very well, and will observe and question as a matter of habit, and will come to a point where you realise something is about to, or may benefit from, a change.

I have made a few suggestions below – situations where the **AIM** approach may be of some help.

Weaning from a swaddle

If you feel it is time for baby to come out of their swaddle, look at their current behaviour and needs and use your knowledge of their temperament and reactions to decide whether you should try a gradual approach – freeing one arm at a time then swaddling around their middle before putting them into a sleeping bag – or whether you feel confident doing it all in one go. Formulate a plan, put it into action and reassess at every stage, making modifications as you go.

> A good tip is to look at how baby uses their hands and arms. If they can reliably grasp and hold an object, often at around three or four months, they are usually ready to come out of their swaddle.

Transitioning to a cot

Most babies start off sleeping in a moses basket, so at some point will need to be moved to a cot, often in a separate room. You will need to assess their sleeping patterns as they are now, where they are sleeping and where they will be sleeping. You could think about the timing, to make sure that nothing else is changing for baby at the same time that would upset them such as a holiday, vaccinations, long days out, visitors or noisy parties or sleepovers.

Then go on to think about how the cot will be different from the moses basket. How will it feel to baby? Is the mattress as soft, or harder (it's usually harder)? Would baby mind this?

> Temporarily placing the moses basket mattress on top of a firmer cot mattress can be a good way of minimising the difference between the two and will make it easier for baby to make the adjustment.

Does baby ever nap or play in the cot? Do they ever drift off to sleep there? If so, this could indicate that they are happy and comfortable there. If not, would it be a good idea to put baby to play there, or put the moses basket in the cot for daytime naps in preparation?

Is the room a different temperature from where they normally sleep? Could that be altered? Are the light levels the same? Might you need blackout blinds? Music/white noise?

How are you feeling about moving baby to another room? Are you confident or anxious? If anxious, what exactly is worrying you? How can you reassure yourself? Are you going to use a baby monitor? If so, do you know how to use it properly? Would it help you to practise by having baby sleep in the cot with the monitor for daytime naps until you are comfortable? If you are really anxious, might a breathing monitor help you relax, or might it make you worse? If you are not using a monitor, are you sure you will be able to hear baby from anywhere in the house?

What will you do if baby's sleep pattern changes? Will you carry on for a few days, monitoring sleep patterns and giving them time to adjust? Will it help you to keep detailed records of their sleep patterns so you can adjust daytime naps until they are settled?

Altering feed intervals

Most babies start off on two- or three-hourly feeds, but there will come a time when you wonder if they are ready to move on to longer intervals, such as feeds every three and a half or four hours, so you might start by assessing the situation.

Are the feeds regular at the moment? Is baby sleeping well during daytime naps and at night? Are they waking up hungry before the feed is due, or are you waking them? If so, how often are they waking up, or acting as if they are hungry before the feed, and for how long before the feed? Do they seem hungry for the feed or not really bothered? If baby is still asleep or playing happily when it is feed time, and not seeming particularly hungry, then that is a good sign that they are ready, or could cope with, a longer interval between feeds, so it might be worth working out a likely schedule, implementing it, recording their response and then re-assessing and modifying if necessary.

If you are unsure about altering the routine, remember that if it goes a bit wrong it is not the end of the world – you can *always* return to your previous routine, which you know works, in order to identify what went wrong and why.

From your records, you may spot a pattern that indicates baby is happy with longer intervals in the mornings but needs the shorter intervals towards the end of the day, or vice versa. Remember, it is all about spotting patterns, and there is no rule that says baby has to have the same feeding intervals throughout the day; it is all about what works for them, and for you.

Adjusting daytime naps

A common question I hear is when will baby drop their daytime naps, or how many hours should they sleep at their age? As I say about every aspect of your baby's routine, there are no shoulds or shouldn'ts. No two babies are alike, and no two families are alike, so ignore what it says in books or guidelines and go with what works for you and your baby.

Assess how your baby is behaving on his current nap regime. Are they calm and content? Are they alert when awake, and tired enough to go to sleep easily? Do the naptimes suit you?

Is baby starting to wake earlier than they used to, and not seeming as sleepy when it is time to nap? If this is the case, it could indicate that they no longer need as much sleep as they used to and that it is time to change the regime.

> Some babies, while no longer needing a sleep, can often benefit from 'quiet time' where they stay in their cot and either just relax, or play quietly with a soft toy or book.

You will know from your notes and experience whether they are naturally more tired in the morning, around the middle of the day or in the afternoon, which will give you guidance as to timings and help you decide if you should drop a nap, shorten all the naps or create one big nap.

You need to consider how changing naptimes will impact your daily routine, your plans and those of your family, as you may have to work around school pick-up and drop-off times.

Are there any groups or activities for you or baby that might be more accessible if you can change naptimes?

When you have investigated all these factors, you can then go on to create a plan to modify naptimes, which you can then implement and see what happens. You may need to reassess and remodify the plan several times before you find a new regime that works for everyone.

Play

As your baby develops, their play requirements will change as their patience levels, boredom levels and physical abilities change. Sometimes you can prepare for this, but most often it ends up with the parent playing catch-up with their baby as they notice a difference in behaviour but don't necessarily understand why it is happening.

While not strictly pre-emptive planning, I feel it is important enough to include play in this section, especially as a certain amount of forethought can make any problems easier to deal with.

The most common problem I come across is boredom, as baby suddenly outgrows their toys and play habits without the parents realising. The first thing they notice is that their baby, who used to play happily on their own, suddenly cries more after shorter play-times. Quite often this is misinterpreted as hunger or teething or wanting to be picked up, but the most usual cause is boredom or frustration. Where they were once happy to lie looking at toys hanging above them, they are now beginning to want to touch and interact with them.

If you notice a change in your baby's behaviour, try assessing the situation from somewhere where they cannot see you, so you get an accurate picture of what is really happening.

Are they looking at the toys for a while, then starting to cry? How long is their concentration span? Are they waving their arms or kicking their legs a lot? Can you see any attempt to touch a toy while looking at it? Are any of the toys within easy reach to encourage their efforts to grab? Are all the toys above them, or are some round the sides? What holds their attention most?

The answers to these questions could reveal that baby is interested for a while but then loses interest and starts crying when they try to touch toys but get nowhere. If you think this is the case, you can modify their immediate environment so that there are toys all around them that they can both touch and kick (people forget that babies love exploring with their feet and toes) to encourage their efforts.

Ask yourself how long baby has been looking at or playing with the same toys. Bearing in mind that babies are what I call 'sensation junkies', and want new and interesting things that they can study and explore to help them make sense of the world, looking at the same toys is just boring. If you think this might be the case, change some of their toys and see what happens. Are they suddenly more interested and happy again?

You don't need to go out and buy a lot of new toys – simply swap in some new toys while putting the old toys away for a week or two. Once they are bored with the new toys, you can bring the old ones out again and they will suddenly have novelty value.

You can also use normal everyday household things for baby to look at and explore. They might be boring for you, but that's only because you have seen them hundreds of times. To a baby who has never seen one before, a brightly coloured stripy sock or piece of used wrapping paper can be spellbinding and keep them occupied for hours.

Knowing your baby will soon get bored with their toys means that you can plan ahead to have new, more interesting toys ready, or spend time finding or borrowing the next stage up from friends or relatives or toy banks.

Be aware, too, that as your baby develops they will be more and more interested in human interaction. As this happens, and baby is less satisfied with toys, they often manage to train parents or carers into picking them up by crying and then end up being carried around or played with to the point where they forget how to play by themselves, making life very difficult for busy parents. It doesn't have to be that way if you are prepared and spend time thinking about how you can interact with your baby without holding them.

Some ways of doing this might be moving baby's play mat or bouncy chair to the kitchen or laundry/utility room so you can chat to them while they play and observe, and you cook or fold clothes. Maybe they could play on the bathroom floor while you have a bath or shower, or bath siblings? Can they roll around on the floor during older children's story time? Or sit in a bouncy chair by the table or in a high chair at the table while you eat your evening meal?

You can keep a special set of toys that baby can play with at key times, maybe older children's toys or shiny (non-lethal!) kitchen implements or wooden spoons that will hold their interest and allow you to get things done.

Assess how their behaviour is linked to their physical position. Do they roll and get stuck? If so, how can you modify their environment to prevent this, or encourage their ability to roll back? Are they bored of playing lying down, but happier when sitting up? If so, what equipment or toys can you use to allow baby to sit up (this frees their hands, so they often enjoy more fiddly toys to play with)? Might they be ready for doorway bouncers, baby seats or jumparoo-type toys?

Once babies start enjoying playing sitting up, it is often a good time to change their bassinet-type pram to a more upright seat if you have not already done so.

6.

How to wind your baby

First things first: **all babies get wind!**

I am stressing this because of the common misconception that breastfed babies don't get wind. They do, all of them, everywhere – there is not a single baby on the planet that does not get wind, whether they are fed from bottles or breast or both! Some babies get more wind than others, and some are easier than others to wind, but they all get it and they all need help to bring it up.

The necessity for stressing this is illustrated beautifully in the case study in Chapter 1 where a health professional, who should have known better, told new parents that a breastfed baby didn't need winding, resulting in their baby being in pain for six weeks, with the parents pushed to the edge of despair.

New parents face a very steep learning curve with each baby they have, and apart from confusion and lack of sleep, the biggest problem they encounter is how to deal with a baby who has wind.

Baby books and health professionals all provide variations on a theme of patting or rubbing baby on the back or lying them over your knee, but they don't provide any sort of in-depth explanations or detailed descriptions, or tackle the issue of why babies are getting the wind in the first place. This is totally understandable because, once you start getting into it, it is a hugely complicated subject, but it just happens to be my favour-ite subject – my 'superpower', if you like.

Most maternity nurses have some sort of speciality, usually based on personal interest. For some it is multiple births; for others it is reflux or premature babies or sleep problems; and so on. For me it is winding, because I see it as *the* key to a contented baby.

A baby in pain from stomach wind can neither feed properly nor sleep well and is therefore much more likely to be fretful and unhappy, a situation which has a knock-on effect on the parents.

Efficient winding can make a huge difference to a baby's health and happiness, allowing routines to be implemented, sleep prob-lems to be addressed, playtimes to be contented and relaxed, and is a vital factor in managing a baby with colic or reflux.

Why do babies get wind?

Babies get wind in the same way we do, by swallowing air along with something we are eating or drinking, and even from swal-lowing our own saliva.

The similarity ends there, though, because when the air ends up in our stomachs we barely feel it, and are easily capable of bringing it up in a fairly controlled manner. In babies it causes pain, and they are unable to bring it up themselves until they are five or six months old.

As babies feed, they must first make contact with the nipple or teat with their tongue and lips, position it so that it is comfortable for them, then start to suck. As they suck they create a vacuum and the lips are pulled tightly around the nipple or teat, creating a seal.

The better the seal, the less air gets into the mouth, so less is swallowed down into the stomach, but air is still getting into the back of the baby's throat as they breathe through their noses, which is why a breastfeeding baby, even with their mouth full of nipple and a seemingly perfect seal, will still get wind.

How well your baby is able to create an efficient seal is determined by their physical ability to manoeuvre their lips and tongue around the nipple or teat, and by their temperament, as to how patient and persistent they are when trying.

As a parent or carer, you can also help your baby get and maintain a better seal by considering the physical, temperamental and environmental circumstances surrounding the feed and using the Assess, Investigate and Modify process to discover if they could be overtired, overly hungry, stressed or in pain, all of which could have a negative impact on feeding.

A good tip is always to try to wind baby before you start feeding, in case they have any wind left over from the last feed that might cause trouble for this feed.

Some babies figure out making the seal and latch on immediately and never have any problems, but others need more time to perfect their technique, and though it is very tempting to start changing bottles and teats and trying to 'fix' things, the best thing you can do is give your baby plenty of time and opportunity to figure it out for themselves.

With both breastfeeding and bottle-feeding, use the **AIM** process to ensure they are well rested and relaxed, and hungry enough to try but not so hungry they get frustrated. Create a comfortable, peaceful environment with few or no distractions and no stresses such as loud noises, people interrupting you, siblings climbing on you or demanding attention.

Remember, they are as new to feeding as you are, but they have instinct on their side and will eventually figure it out. However, they will get there much quicker if you provide them with optimum conditions. I know it is difficult to juggle a new baby with everyday life and other children, but it is definitely worth investing the time early on to get feeding as calm and efficient as possible in order to prevent problems such as excessive wind later on.

Apart from air that gets into the baby's mouth via their nose, the other main reason air is swallowed is that baby stops sucking and breaks the seal they have built up and then goes back to feeding again.

This can happen because they are getting full, because they are uncomfortable with wind and because they are not really hungry or are getting distracted, but it can also be because the milk is flowing too fast for them to be able to cope with. They need to settle to a nice, easy breathe-suck-swallow rhythm, and this can become interrupted by fast-flowing milk pooling or hitting the back of their throat. If you think this might be the case, it is worth trying a slower-flow teat for a while, if bottle feeding, or, if breastfeeding, try expressing a little breastmilk before the feed to reduce initial flow, just until they become more practised at feeding.

NOTE Babies do not get wind from being bottle-fed in a lying down position.

This is a complete myth, and has led to many an uncomfortable bottle-feeding session with a parent struggling to try to feed baby in a sitting position. Please don't do this: you are just making life more difficult than it needs to be. If a breastfed baby can feed lying down, so can a bottle-fed baby. Experiment with cushions and pillows, like a breastfeeder would, and snuggle down comfortably with your baby, relax and enjoy it. The only babies that benefit from being fed in a more upright position are babies suffering from reflux, because being upright keeps milk and acid away from the stomach valve, and is nothing to do with the fact that baby is being fed with a bottle.

> Don't stop feeding to wind baby every ounce, or every few minutes, as the more times the seal is broken the more opportunity there is for baby to swallow wind. Leave them to stop naturally unless they are prone to being sick or you suspect reflux.

Anatomy of a baby's stomach

Generally people know that babies have tiny stomachs and need frequent feeds, but beyond that, most expectant or new parents are told little else, which is a pity because a few basic facts can greatly help to understand winding.

The baby's stomach is often referred to as being the size of an almond and many people imagine a little smooth almond-shaped thing below the ribcage, in the middle, with the oesophagus joining it at the top. In fact, baby's stomach is much more of a kidney bean shape, with one end bigger than the other, and the oesophagus joins it from the side.

It is also much bigger than the 5ml to 7ml (less than one fluid ounce) that is sometimes quoted as its capacity and has recently been shown through ultrasound to be 16-20ml, but even this is just an average. I have seen many newborns drink more than 20ml on their first day. I have seen many newborns quite happily polish off a 90ml (3oz) bottle!

The big end of the stomach is not central, but over to the baby's left, and most of it is up underneath the ribcage with just the bottom third of the small end curling round to the centre. The oesophagus enters the stomach from the baby's right, a little below the top of the stomach.

What should also be explained is that the lining of the stomach is not smooth.

The stomach is very elastic, which allows it to expand as it is filled with food, but this means that for most of the time it is in its relaxed, more shrivelled state, leaving the stomach lining ridged and pleated. Most of the ridges run longitudinally – along the length of the stomach – but they are not straight: there are a lot of folds, bends and 'S' shapes, all of which means that there are lots of nooks and crannies where little bubbles of wind can get stuck.

Bubbles of air in the stomach behave in exactly the same way as bubbles anywhere else: they always try to rise. Imagine a bottle of carbonated water, in which the bubbles are rising. If you pat the bottle, more bubbles are dislodged and rise faster, and with some babies (though rarely, in my experience) this is all that is required to release bubbles of wind.

This is the simplified version of winding, but bearing in mind what you now know about the physiology of your baby's stomach, a much better analogy would be to imagine one of the 'Marble in a Maze' games where the marble (bubble) gets stuck in corners and you have to manoeuvre and manipulate the maze (your baby's body) many times in order to release it.

Even this can be further complicated by the fact that your baby will be wriggling, you may be inexperienced, and, if your baby is crying or screaming, their stomach and abdomen are tensed up to the point where it is virtually impossible to get any wind to come up. This is why I ask you to use the **AIM** process to get yourself and your baby as calm as possible before you start feeding.

Winding positions and techniques: key points

You can use any of the following techniques on any baby. Just think about what is going on in that particular situation, bearing in mind that baby's winding needs can be very different depending on the circumstances of the moment, their temperament and their medical/physical state.

I find it helpful to think of winding methods as being either *active* or *passive*.

The more active methods can be used on a happy, calm baby who isn't stressed by being handled and is not prone to being sick. These methods are also useful for keeping a sleepy baby awake.

The more passive methods can be useful for an overtired baby, or one who is upset, ill or suffers from reflux, or simply when you don't want to do anything to stimulate your baby, such as during a night feed.

Most of the following techniques can be modified to be either more active or more passive by changing the speed or smoothness of your movements and by adjusting noise, light and activity levels in the environment. For example, if you are aiming for active winding, you can be chatting to your baby, moving around the house, with lots going on around you, and your movements can be brisk and firm. Whereas if you want winding to be calming, then you can use the same movements but make the room dark and/or quiet, don't talk to baby and make all movements extra-slow and smooth.

Just as a hint for when you are tired and stressed, I have marked those techniques that are particularly suitable for *passive* winding with a P.

The following points may help you understand some of the techniques and positions, and give you a few tips as well:

- You are always aiming to elongate your baby's body, which will help to straighten the kinks in the stomach lining and in turn help to free bubbles.

- You need to keep you baby's head lifted so that they look straight ahead, not down. This opens the airways and helps straighten the oesophagus and takes pressure off the stomach valve.

- Do not apply anything other than the gentlest pressure (like the weight of your hand or their own body weight) to baby's stomach.

- If a technique or position is not producing results after two minutes, it probably isn't working, so stop and try something else.

- For everything you do when winding, try to hold the image of your baby's stomach in your mind and imagine what effect your actions might have on an air bubble trapped somewhere inside it (remember the marble maze).

- It is very common for babies to bring up a little (or a lot) of milk when they burp. This is simply due to the valve at the top of the stomach being a bit inefficient at keeping milk down while at the same time allowing wind up. It can make feeding and winding very messy, but it improves with age as the valve matures. On its own it does not mean your baby has reflux, so don't panic.

- As much as possible, try to wind in a position that allows you to see your baby's face because, though some babies produce nice, loud, satisfying burps, a lot of the time the burps can be very, very quiet and breathy and easily missed, so it does help to watch their throat and mouth as you can often see when baby is burping even if you can't hear it.

- Remember that bubbles rise, so after each different position you try, always return baby to the starting position for at least thirty seconds to allow any bubbles you have released to rise to the top of the stomach where they can be burped up.

- There is a pattern to a baby's burps. The first one is usually the biggest and most likely to cause milk return, and is often almost instantaneously followed by smaller 'aftershocks'. There will usually then be a few or many other smaller burps, so don't assume your baby has no more wind just because they have done two big burps. It will take time to get to know your baby's unique wind pattern, so observe and learn.

Starting position (P)

When I watch inexperienced parents trying to wind, I frequently see baby being sat on a lap and held in a round-shouldered, slumping position.

This can actually prevent wind from coming up, and can also place pressure on the stomach and make it much more likely that baby will be sick, especially if they suffer from reflux.

> Always have at least one muslin or burp cloth at hand in case the winding triggers spit-up.

The trick is to get baby sitting up straight, but this involves holding their head. I often hear new parents or relatives worry that they will hurt their baby when they try to hold their head up, so let's address that first.

Have your baby sitting on your lap facing whichever way feels comfortable. If baby is facing right, place your right thumb and either first or middle finger on the cheekbones on either side of the face, directly in front of baby's ears. This gives you somewhere solid to hold which won't damage or hurt baby in any way, but be careful not to hold the jaw joint below as that may be uncomfortable for baby. Keeping your fingers in place, lengthen your hand to a flattened 'U' or 'V' shape and rest the heel of your hand on baby's chest, which keeps your hand away from baby's throat. If you then place your little finger under baby's armpit at the same time as locking your elbow into your waist, you will find you have an extremely stable grip.

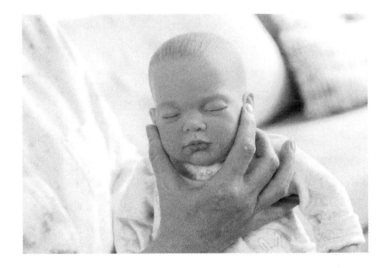

If you then cradle your left hand around baby's lower back, and press in gently while at the same time pushing back slightly with the hand holding baby's head, you will find that baby naturally sits up, which helps straighten out their stomach and windpipe, allowing more effective winding.

If at any time you want to remove the hand from the back to rub or pat, just tilt baby very slightly forward, shifting more of their weight into your face-supporting hand, creating a very safe position. It is worth trying this position and experimenting with it until you feel confident.

I call this the **start position**, and it is the very first thing I do when winding any baby. Not only can it help bring up wind, but it also provides such a secure hold that from there you can safely move baby around into many other winding positions.

Babies have a habit of suddenly jerking backward, so this hold is particularly useful for catching their head in this situation because, with practice, your hand can move extremely quickly from the base of the spine to support the head.

Patting

A quick word about patting. Everyone pats their baby's back, including me. Truthfully, I have no idea if it actually does anything useful. Maybe it does sometimes dislodge bubbles. I know it can be calming for babies; it certainly doesn't do any harm. I once had a client who told me that I was not allowed to pat the baby because a midwife had told her it causes brain damage (totally untrue, by the way), but it was so ingrained a habit that I couldn't stop. My advice is pat if you want to and don't if you don't, but certainly don't worry about it.

When sitting baby up on your lap, it can help their stability and your control to gently trap their dangling legs between yours, because it allows their body to remain straight when you start moving them into different positions.

Up-rub (P)

Hold baby in the starting position, then rub your hand from the base of the spine up to the top. This is not a 'rub up and down' motion – you are just rubbing **upward**, and the aim is to press firmly enough to straighten baby's spine a little, like a gentle Mexican wave of straightness. When you get to the top of the spine, gently allow baby's body to relax to where it was before you started (not slumping forward, because we want to avoid any sudden pressure on the valve at the top of the stomach, especially with reflux babies as it can lead to baby being sick).

I usually count slowly to three for each rub, wait for another count of three and repeat five to ten times. The wait in between rubs allows wind to come up, so remember to watch their face in case they burp quietly.

Tilting (P)

As you hold baby securely in the starting position, very slowly tilt them away from you, sideways, keeping the head supported and

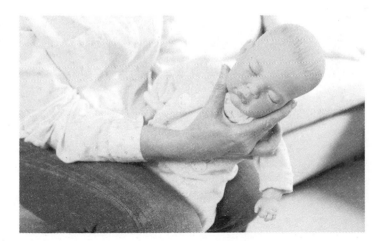

the body straight. It may feel a little insecure, but remember that you can hold baby quite firmly with the cheekbone grip without hurting them.

Think of it as a slow, flowing, t'ai chi movement. You can tilt them a little way or all the way over until they are horizontal (wherever you are comfortable), then hold them there for two or three seconds. Then, just as slowly, bring them back up to the centre. You can repeat the movement, but this time tilt baby towards your body.

I usually tilt away from and towards me three or four times, then hold them still in the centre for ten to twenty seconds before trying some up-rubs.

Tipping (P)

The same tilt can be done backward and forward, with the difference being that you need to move your hand slightly to support the head as you tip them backward. Keep your little finger and ring finger cradling baby's lower back, along with your thumb, but twist your hand slightly so that your first and/or middle finger point upward towards baby's head and neck.

Those two fingers are more than enough to support a baby's head, even if they are only touching just above the top of the neck. Practise with tiny backward tilts until you are confident. Remember to keep their body straight, especially when tipping them forward, because if you allow their body to collapse and their spine to curl, you will be compressing their stomach and risking them being sick.

If your baby suffers from reflux, it is best to avoid winding positions that place direct pressure on the stomach or fold them at the waist as this is much more likely to make them sick.

Once you have mastered both tilting and tipping, you can amalgamate the two moves to create a slow, smooth, continuous circular sequence – forward, side, back, side – which can be very calming for babies.

Over shoulder (P)

Remember that the aim is to elongate baby's body to straighten out any kinks, and using the shoulder can be a good way of doing this. Hold baby under both armpits, raise them up and place them over your shoulder with their head and arms dangling down your back, then slowly bring them slightly down the front of your shoulder until their head is being supported on your shoulder. If you then bring up the arm of the shoulder they are on you can hold them safely in place with the hand on the upper back, leaving their body dangling and your other hand free.

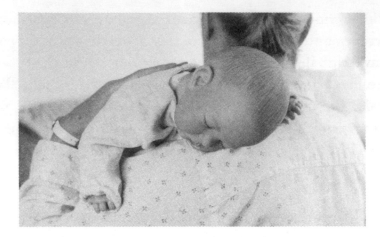

In this position, their body is being gently stretched by gravity and the pressure placed on their stomach is being created by their own body weight, so you know it won't hurt them. Simply leave them in this position for thirty seconds. Sometimes this is enough to bring up wind without doing anything further, but if nothing happens, then you can try the up-rub movement but with hardly any pressure (remember, there is already pressure on their stomach from your shoulder, and any more could result in vomiting).

Over knees

The aim of this position is *not* to try to squeeze air out of the stomach; it is simply a change of position which might cause a trapped bubble to be released.

There are two ways of doing this, depending on how your baby is reacting and how full they are.

To start with, place baby face down over your knees, with arms extended forwards on either side of the head, and the head supported on your leg. Now stop and look at the position of their stomach in relation to your legs.

Is their stomach resting on your thigh, or is it in the gap between your thighs?

Now think about what is going on with your baby.

Are they prone to being sick? Is their tummy very full? Have they done any burps yet? Are they in pain from the wind, and upset or tense? If this is the case, then you should be aiming to have baby's stomach over the gap *between* your thighs so that there is no pressure at all on the stomach that might cause pain or regurgitation. Obviously the size and shape of your thighs will make a difference, so you can either move baby down nearer to your knees, or up nearer to your body, or you can just open your legs a little to create a gap. However, I do mean a little gap, enough so that there is nothing for the stomach to press on but narrow enough for the lower abdomen (the nappy area) to be supported by the other thigh, otherwise you may hurt their back.

The up-rub is useful here, as it is very calming. The aim is just to leave baby in this position from thirty seconds up to five minutes. Then sit them up into the starting position.

If baby is not prone to being sick, not in pain and not overfull, or has already done one burp, you can try moving baby so that there is no gap and their stomach is gently resting on part of your thigh.

This added pressure can help dislodge bubbles, and up-rub or patting may also help. Leave them there for up to five minutes before returning them to the starting position.

This position, relaxed over the knees, can also be useful if baby is constipated, as the gentle pressure plus the rise and fall of their own breathing can act as a gentle massage for the lower intestines.

Put down/pick up

This is so simple yet so effective, and really can work miracles with stubborn wind. I have found myself in a situation many times where I am trying and failing to get a baby to burp, I have tried everything and am rubbing and patting and getting frustrated, then I remember this.

Quite simply, put baby down on their back and leave them alone for five minutes, then return them to the starting position and see if anything comes up.

Again, this is not for when baby is very full or suffers from reflux, but in most other situations it is fine – just keep an eye on them and pick them up quickly if they look as if they may be sick or are uncomfortable.

Remember that a baby's body needs to be relaxed in order for wind to come up, but when you are working on trying to get them to burp and it isn't succeeding, baby can get tired of being handled, so they often enjoy a bit of peace and quiet, and while they are lying down, moving gently, bubbles are being dislodged and moving to new positions. Then when you sit baby up again and give the bubbles time to rise, baby is more likely to burp for you.

It can be uncomfortable for a reflux baby to be laid flat on their backs too soon after feeding, but you can still utilise this put down/pick up technique by putting them in a baby bouncer. This way, they are held safely in a relaxed position, can still gently move their bodies around but are more upright, which will keep milk and acid away from the stomach valve.

I put babies down like this on my lap, on a sofa, on the floor, in a moses basket, in a pram or in a cot under a mobile. I remember one baby who got so annoyed when I persisted in trying to wind him (so I could continue the feed), that he would actually growl at me and didn't want to be on my knee or even near me, but I learnt, by trial and error, that if I put him on a blanket in the conservatory where he could watch the trees, he would lie quite happily, and when he began to wriggle and squirm, I would pick him up and he would burp.

This is also a very good way to wind baby if the parent or carer is tired or getting stressed for whatever reason, because it requires no effort or frustrating movements such as rubbing and patting and gives you the chance to calm down in between winding bouts.

You can repeat this action as many times as you like, and can use it between other winding positions or techniques.

> If you are part way through a feed and unsure if baby still has wind, try them at the breast or with the bottle again. They will soon show you if they are still uncomfortable by wriggling, writhing, crying or starting to feed then pulling off again. Don't shy away from trying for fear of getting it wrong!

Swaddling

Not usually thought of as a winding technique, but it does work for some babies. If you have been trying to wind and are getting nowhere, you can try a good firm swaddle, even if you never use one at any other time. All it does is straighten out baby's body beautifully, applies a little safe pressure to the whole torso and helps baby relax.

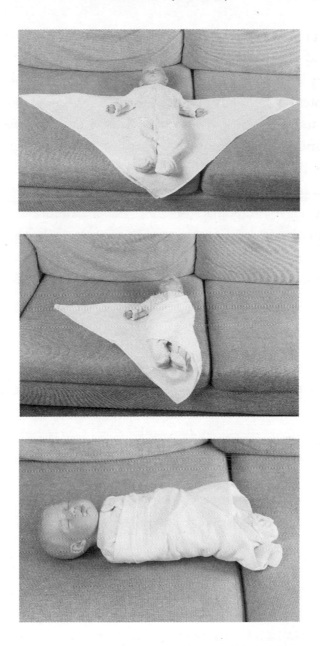

Use a muslin, cot sheet or cotton swaddle (not stretchy) to wrap baby snugly in a straight position, aiming to cover the body, not the legs. Once baby is wrapped, pick them up and hold them upright against your own chest or shoulder, keeping them as upright and straight as possible for a few minutes, and try the up-rub. You can also walk around with them like this, or go up and down stairs to see if any bubbles are dislodged.

Alternatively, if you are winding a baby that is already swaddled (if they have woken from a sleep) and you can't get the wind up, then try unswaddling them and see if that helps.

You can also apply all the other winding techniques or positions with a swaddled baby, as long as the swaddle isn't so tight that baby cannot comfortably bend in the middle. It is worth a try, especially if your baby is getting upset and might benefit from a calming swaddle.

Dislodging difficult wind

Although some rare babies are very easy to wind, most are not and most parents will, at some point, come up against the really tricky burps that just won't come up. This is where you need to become more proactive and inventive.

Experienced parents will know the frustration of having battled to get baby to bring up their wind for what feels like hours, only to have them burp easily the second they are handed to someone else. It feels like a conspiracy, and can lead the other person to claim, smugly, that 'they have the knack'. Quite simply, winding is caused by the movement involved in passing the baby, dislodging a hidden or trapped bubble.

Frustrating though this is, we can use it to our advantage by incorporating it into our own winding strategies by getting up and moving around.

The simplest method is just to walk around. The over-the-shoulder position is good because it is very secure. As long as baby's head and arms are slightly over the shoulder and hanging down your back, you can safely hold them with one hand (the same hand as the supporting shoulder), holding baby in place behind their shoulder blades. This stops baby slipping down, and you can then adjust your grip so that thumb and fingers are on either side of baby's neck to stop the head slipping.

This one-handed grip means that your other hand is free to steady yourself as you get up, and hold onto banisters if negotiating stairs.

Once up, and you are sure baby is secure, you can pace up and down, dance around to music, go up and down stairs or potter around the house doing things one-handed. I know from experience that, as the saying goes, 'a watched pot never boils', so it seems at times that the burps come up once you stop trying so hard, so walking around is definitely worth a go.

A good tip is to try even more movement by sitting on the edge of your bed or on a gym ball, and bouncing. This is remarkably therapeutic if you yourself are stressed or tense, and babies seem to love it too.

A more *passive* version is to sit in a rocking chair if you have one. Hold baby over your shoulder or upright on your knee and rock. You are still introducing more movement to the winding, but it is much less stimulating.

Distraction

If you are trying to wind a baby that is distressed by pain, hunger or overtiredness, then sometimes a change of scene can be a very helpful distraction, and there has been many a time when I have had to go and find a distraction to finish winding. Remember, baby has to be calm for their wind to come up, so anything that takes their mind off whatever is upsetting them will help immensely.

Kitchens with bright downlights and shiny utensils and pans can be good, as are windows, especially those near trees or bushes that might move in the wind.

Bathrooms are often excellent distractions, because baby spends little time there so everything is new and interesting, and I have found myself winding while perched on the side of the bath on more than one occasion. There are shiny taps and towel rails, sparkly mirrors and tiles, and you can run the taps for extra distraction.

Going to find other people or a television can be a good distraction for baby, and can also be a great de-stressing activity for a stressed parent.

Once you are confident that you can hold baby securely, you can go and wind anywhere, even outside.

> Get to know your own baby's particular winding pattern, so you can have a good idea of when they have brought up all their wind. Some may only need to do two or three big burps, while others do a big burp followed by several small ones, or have lots of tiny bubbles to bring up.

Tools

As well as positions and techniques, there are a few things that can help bring up wind.

GRIPE WATER AND OTHER TREATMENTS The first thing most people think of to help with trapped wind is gripe water. This is a very old-fashioned remedy, and used to contain alcohol which acted as a relaxant and did, according to my own mother, work quite well. Nowadays the alcohol has been removed and it is just water flavoured with herbs, and in my experience, does little if anything to help.

It helps to know that wind is a physical problem. Bubbles are stuck and need help to be released, so herbs will not make any difference.

The act of swallowing sends liquid down the oesophagus, and as the valve opens to allow liquid into the stomach, it is also a good opportunity for wind to escape, therefore sometimes small amounts – sips – of liquid can help, but any liquid will do. Cooled boiled water is as effective as gripe water, or anything else, but remember that at the same time as baby is swallowing the liquid, they can also be swallowing air, causing more problems, which is why I rarely use this technique.

The only winding remedies I do ever use are ones which contain a chemical called simethicone. It is inert, so it cannot be absorbed into baby's body, making it very safe. It acts on the surface tension of bubbles and makes small bubbles join together to form big ones, which are then easier to dislodge and be released. In the UK the product name is Infacol, and it is one of the few things I make sure I take to every job because it is so useful. It is not a miracle cure for every baby, and on some seems to make little difference, but on others it can bring amazing results.

As with everything I use on babies, I tried it on myself first by taking some after drinking sparkling water, and I definitely felt the difference. Instructions advise giving it before every feed, but I rarely do that as it works within a couple of minutes, so I only give it whenever I feel the winding is getting too difficult, which can be every feed, once or twice a day or very occasionally, depending on baby's needs.

PACIFIER As I've mentioned, the act of swallowing can help wind come up, so sometimes giving the baby a pacifier to suck on can help, especially as it usually relaxes baby – which is always the goal in winding. You can pop in a pacifier and then either leave baby in one position for a while, or continue winding with it in. Not always successful, but definitely worth a try.

SWADDLES As I've already mentioned, you can use any piece of cloth as a swaddle, but my all-time favourite swaddle is called the Miracle Blanket and I love it because it is cotton, it is cheap, it washes and dries easily and is the most versatile swaddle I have come across. You can swaddle your baby for winding even if you don't use it at any other time, even with older babies, especially if you leave their arms free.

BABY SLING/CARRIER The other thing you can use to help with winding is any sling or baby carrier that holds the baby upright (not wrapped around your body at an angle). I use this when baby is very upset, as they almost always find it calming, and I can use movement to try to dislodge bubbles without over-handling baby. I have also used it on occasion when a baby has fallen fast asleep without burping. I just pop them in the sling and continue with my day until I hear the burp I am waiting for.

How to become an efficient winder

Winding can be the most frustrating aspect of baby care, and I have known many people dread feeding because of the accompanying winding, but it doesn't have to be that way.

I have given you a starting point and some techniques that are very effective, but it may help you to know that I was not born knowing how to wind, nor did anyone teach me. I learnt exactly the same way as any parent would – through experience. The fact that I have been 'experiencing' winding for my whole adult working life has just given me more time to think about it.

I questioned what was happening inside baby; what I was doing; how it made me feel; how it might be making baby feel; and, most importantly, I experimented.

The fastest and best way to become a good parent is to educate yourself and then use that knowledge, and your instincts, to try different ways of doing things. The process of trial and error is your biggest and best friend. Use it. Don't be afraid you will get it wrong. You might make mistakes, but they are rectifiable, usually very quickly, and you can always learn something from them.

DON'T BE AFRAID OF WINDING Turn it into a game. Men are particularly good at this when I present winding as a challenge, and very quickly start coming up with their own ideas, and there are plenty of couples I know where the dad is the one who can get the stubborn burps up and give mum a welcome break.

Use my tips as a starting point and go on from there. Invent your own positions and techniques, discover your own distractions, find out what suits you and works best for your baby. To very new parents it can seem impossible, but I promise you that with thought and practice, you will quickly become a competent winder.

> The trick to effective winding is to use lots of different positions and techniques to dislodge the bubbles, so if something is not working after thirty seconds, stop and try something else.

7.

Useful tools and equipment

During the **AIM** problem-solving process, you will work your way through **Assessment** and **Investigation** and will then arrive at the **Modification** phase, where you will begin to devise plans and strategies to resolve some of the problems you have identified.

This will involve thinking about every aspect of baby's care and daily routine, about what you can modify and how. Something you will find invaluable in this process is a 'baby behaviour toolkit'.

By this I mean a selection of equipment and personalised strategies that you can draw upon time and time again when searching for ways to improve yours and baby's situation, whatever the problem.

Equipment

These are things that you can either buy or make that can be used to soothe or distract baby or make them more comfortable, enabling you to change a behaviour or a reaction, and include:

- pacifier/dummy
- swaddle cloth
- music/sound apps/white noise
- comforters/toys
- bottle/teat
- sling
- yoga ball/gym ball

Pacifier/dummy

This is the single most useful tool you can have, but it is also the most underused, misunderstood, misused and most feared.

There is a great deal of strong feeling surrounding the use of pacifiers among parents (and friends, relatives, in-laws and complete strangers), the most common expression being, 'I don't want to use a pacifier because I don't want my baby to get addicted to it', quickly followed by, 'I saw a four-/five-/six-/seven-year-old with one in the street and they looked awful'.

Pacifiers do not create an addiction.

To clarify: they do not jump up of their own accord, leap into your baby's mouth and then refuse to leave. The only way for a pacifier to get into a baby's mouth is if someone puts it there and leaves it there. After a while baby gets used to it, expects it and protests when it doesn't get it, and the parents or carers give in and provide the pacifier, so reinforcing the habit until a behavioural addiction is created.

This may sound blunt, but it needs to be to get the point across, and it is something I have had to remind myself of and deal with on every single job I have gone to over the years, because I am just as guilty as any parent. I start off using a pacifier sensibly and carefully, then gradually, as I get more tired or baby gets more persistent, I slip into lazy ways and reach for the pacifier as a quick and easy fix.

The difference between myself and parents is that my experience has shown me first-hand how quickly a bad habit can be created and how hard it can then be to break it, and the last thing I want is to create a problem for my clients.

YOUR INNER VOICE I have an inner voice that constantly monitors all aspects of my baby care, questioning my every action; e.g. does baby really need the pacifier? When did they last have it? For how long? Am I being lazy? Am I giving it automatically whenever baby seems unsettled? Should I be trying something else first, such as winding or a new toy or a distraction? Might baby settle if I leave them to try for a while without the pacifier? Is what I am doing going to be unhelpful for the parents in the long term, after I have left?

If you are worried you are overusing the pacifier, leave yourself Post-it notes around the house to remind yourself to think before you use it.

Some people are naturally great parents (or just very lucky!), but for most parents or carers the difference between competence and chaos can be that internal voice – questioning, intelligent, thoughtful and open-minded. It is this voice I want to help you develop to the point where you know exactly what you are doing and why and what the consequence could be both short term and long term, and if there was one gift I could give any parent it would be this voice.

YOUR BABY'S NEED TO SUCK As I mentioned in Chapter 2, the absolute favourite thing a baby does is to suck. It enables survival in the form of milk, as well as comfort and relief from tiredness, pain, hunger, wind, upset/crying, fear, shock and even boredom. If used wisely, a pacifier can bring that same relief and comfort to many situations parents encounter during everyday interaction with baby, and can have particular relevance to problem-solving situations.

Examples of a pacifier being used as a tool to address a particular problem:

- TEMPORARY RELIEF from hunger or tiredness when you are trying to alter baby's routine and change feed or sleep times. While sometimes it is possible to distract or cuddle a baby for sufficient time to allow the feed or sleep to be moved, at other times baby may be too hungry or overtired to cope without further comfort.

- INTERVENTION and comfort if baby is in meltdown from being overtired or over-handled. This is when baby needs some instant soothing and, apart from a feed, a pacifier is the quickest, most reliable way to achieve this.

- COMFORT from pain if baby has reflux before, during and after a feed. Reflux babies are in frequent or constant pain from stomach acid rising and burning the throat, and so need as much comfort as we can possibly give them. Sucking on a pacifier is physically and emotionally soothing and can greatly improve feed times for everyone. If baby is distressed by wind during and after a feed, a pacifier helps calm baby, allowing winding to take place. If baby is in so much pain from wind that they cannot relax enough to be winded or to continue the feed, a pacifier can provide the comfort a baby needs to allow effective winding to take place.

- SLEEP SETTLER as a temporary way to settle a baby to sleep, particularly those under four weeks. The first few weeks with a new baby are a time of massive adjustment and confusion for both parents and baby, and it can take a while to get to know your baby well enough to understand what they are trying to tell you. It can make sense to use the pacifier to help comfort the baby while the parents' skills are growing and improving, and to give them a bit of breathing space in which to relax and enjoy their baby at the same time.

- DISTRACTION and comfort during injections and medical procedures, and invaluable during hospital stays. Your baby will have no understanding of why they are in strange surroundings, being held and manipulated by strangers and experiencing discomfort and perhaps pain, and the most comforting thing would be a cuddle and something to suck. However, as doctors and nurses do their jobs it may not be practical for the baby to be held, in which case a pacifier is the very best way to comfort your little one.

- STIMULATE SUCKING REFLEX in small and premature or ill babies. Often recommended by health professionals in hospitals, a pacifier can be a profound source of comfort, especially if baby is in an incubator and has little physical contact with parents.

- TEMPORARY SILENCING during important situations such as weddings and christenings, and on trains and planes where your usual methods are impractical. Sometimes a pacifier is the one thing that can make a social situation bearable, especially as routines are often upset and surroundings unfamiliar for baby. They have the added advantage of being able to be offered or given by anybody, and so allow others to help calm baby while parents deal with siblings or other duties, and maybe even have a few minutes to socialise themselves. As for travelling on a plane, if I am asked to fly with a baby my standard answer is 'yes, but only if I am allowed to use a pacifier', as the thought of travelling without one is just too awful to contemplate.

- TRAVELLING Temporary relief and comfort from pain, wind, hunger, tiredness and boredom when travelling by car and when no other safe action is possible. This can be a necessary safety measure to allow parents to concentrate on driving rather than trying to turn round and quieten a crying or screaming baby.

Get into the habit of having a clean pacifier that is always left in the car. Even if you never use it, it will be there for emergencies.

- AID TO EXHAUSTED PARENTS Relief from a screaming baby when the parents are exhausted and have nothing left to give, or are in pain, ill, upset or trying to deal with siblings or urgent matters. There is so much stress and pressure involved in caring for a new baby that the parents owe it to themselves, for their health and their sanity, to give themselves a break when they need one, and a pacifier can give you the peace and quiet you need and deserve.

- COPING STRATEGY Valuable in cases of postnatal depression or anxiety. In a situation such as this the priority must be alleviating as much stress and pressure as possible for the mother or father suffering from depression or anxiety, and nothing is as stress-inducing as a crying or screaming baby.

- FEED DELAY TACTIC Used as temporary relief from hunger if baby wakes early for a feed or if bottle/mum isn't quite ready, particularly during the night. A hungry baby doesn't understand that food is on the way; they just know they are hungry and it is a kindness sometimes to give them temporary relief until the food arrives and can stop a sensitive baby getting so wound up they can't feed properly. Keeping baby quiet for a few minutes also gives the parent the mental space to prepare either themselves or the bottle efficiently, without rushing, plus it can prevent levels of noise that might disturb noise-sensitive sleeping siblings or partners.

- LATCH AID FOR BREASTFEEDING Used to trick a baby to latch onto the nipple during breastfeeding. Sometimes when breastfeeding baby becomes frustrated by hunger, wind, overtiredness or reflux and may refuse even to try to latch on, but if you give them a pacifier they will often calm down and relax. If you hold them to the breast in latching position and wait until baby is very relaxed and sucking calmly, it is often possible gently and smoothly to slip the pacifier out of baby's mouth at the same time as presenting the nipple, which they then instinctively take.

- **GAIN MOMENTS OF CALM** I always take a pacifier when I go to get baby's passport photos taken, because if they get upset they can have it to calm down. Then, if you warn the photographer to be ready, you can pop out the pacifier, the picture is snapped and the pacifier is replaced before baby has the chance to get upset. This works just as well for normal family snaps and for professional portraits.

If a pacifier is not available, a clean little finger (with a short nail) can be used. Place it upside down in baby's mouth so the soft pad of your little finger is touching the roof of baby's mouth. This is also good for people who are worried about overusing a pacifier, because you cannot put it in and walk away or leave it in when baby sleeps.

UNDERSTAND WHY YOU ARE USING THE PACIFIER If you understand exactly *why* you are using the pacifier and constantly monitor yourself, it is much easier to use it for the duration of that specific situation only and not get yourself and baby into bad habits.

If you do think your baby is becoming overly reliant on the pacifier, then you can immediately take steps to reduce the frequency and duration of use by instigating other comforts or distractions before a habit is firmly established.

TIPS FOR SENSIBLE PACIFIER USE

- Think carefully about why you are using a pacifier.

- Discuss with your partner or anyone helping to care for your baby exactly in what situation a pacifier may be used and for how long, and make an easily accessible list of situations to avoid confusion or argument.

- Do not leave the pacifier in baby's mouth once a situation has been resolved, e.g. if you use it to help settle baby, always remove it once they have fallen asleep. Failure to remove it leads to the most common cause of sleep disturbance – baby crying for parents to come and replace the pacifier when it falls out – and trust me when I say this can be a soul-destroying way to spend your night!

- Before using a pacifier, ask yourself if there is anything else you could try first: winding, cuddling, distraction, and so on. Notice when you reach for it automatically.

- Remember, you can reserve pacifier use for specific occasions. For example, I had one client who only ever used it in the car when she was on her own with baby; another who used it when her baby was in hospital for two weeks, but then slowly weaned him off it when they were settled back at home; and a third who used it just to help baby bring up wind because that was when he got most distressed.

- Remember that the reason we give a baby a pacifier is because they are unable to give themselves any form of comfort. As they get older and can reliably bring their hand or a toy to their mouths, they are capable of comforting themselves. This usually happens at around five or six months, and at this stage I start gradually reducing the use of a pacifier.

- Unless there are medical reasons for continuing pacifier use, such as illness or reflux, I use six months as a rough cut-off date and advise parents to stop or drastically reduce usage at this age, as after six months babies can become very resistant, persistent, stubborn and loud!

It may seem as if I am trying to persuade you to use pacifiers, but I promise you that is not the case. I only want to try to help you understand the pros and cons involved, and to encourage you to consider whether or not to use a pacifier based on fact and thought, and not on a knee-jerk reaction that may be fuelled by the misinformed and sensationalised mess that usually surrounds the subject.

Swaddles

Swaddling seems to be another subject that attracts strong opinions. It is also a wonderfully useful, much underrated tool – in fact, it is my all-time favourite, simply because babies love them. If your baby is well fed and well winded, the swaddle is a warm, comfortable, portable hug that helps them go to sleep quicker and stay asleep for longer, and who doesn't want that?

However, it must be used correctly. If your baby is hungry or uncomfortable or in pain from wind, the swaddle can become a prison and they hate it. Whenever I go to a client who tells me their baby hates being swaddled, I usually find on investigation that the baby is insufficiently winded and in pain. The other common problem is that the swaddle is way too loose, and baby is partially restricted but not comfortably snug – much like when we get tangled up in a duvet or bed sheet. Once fed, winded and swaddled, every baby I have ever come across has relaxed and been content. Some might have a few seconds' struggle as they settle and get used to the sensation; then they love it.

RISKS The other frequent comment is that it causes hip problems. Let me reassure you: it is highly unlikely that a safe and sensible swaddle will do any harm!

If a baby was a breech birth, or has a family history of hip problems, and *if* you swaddled them like an Egyptian mummy with their legs straight and pressed together, there would be a *slight* chance that any already existing hip problems may take a little longer to resolve themselves. Even then, you would have to leave the baby swaddled for excessive hours a day over a prolonged period of time for a problem to arise. The aim of the swaddle is to gently restrain the baby's arms so whatever swaddle you use, just make sure that the hips and legs are left with plenty of room to move.

There are many makes of swaddle on the market in the UK, and I have not come across a single one where the recommended use would lead to it being tightened in such a way as to cause hip problems, so unless a paediatrician addressing hip problems has specifically warned you against them, I would seriously urge you to consider their use.

BENEFITS On jobs where I am allowed to swaddle babies, I usually have them waking only once in the night from the first week onward, and sleeping through the majority of the night by eight weeks. This is not down to pacifier use, or any sort of crying or sleep training at all, and it's not because I am a 'baby whisperer'. It is down to a baby care routine that meets all baby's needs, the three most important factors being a full tummy, no wind and finally, comfort and security while they sleep, which is what the swaddle provides.

STARTLE REFLEX In the womb, the baby's body is held snug and secure by the mother's body, but once born a new baby has no control over their limbs. As their nervous system develops, their arms and legs jerk around uncontrollably, preventing them from settling off to sleep and waking them once they are asleep. Their hands may also smack their own faces, and both arms and legs (along with the bottom jaw) can be subject to juddering movements that can look as if baby is suffering from a spasm. This is totally normal and very common, and resolves itself within a few weeks, but it is worrying to see and can sometimes be quite severe. A nice, snug swaddle hugs the baby's arms to their body, preventing the startle reflex from disturbing them whilst they sleep.

COMFORT Many parents instinctively sense their baby's need for security, holding them firmly and cradling them to their chest, which works wonderfully, especially as baby can also feel the parent's heartbeat and body warmth. This is also why babies sleep so well in someone's arms. Cuddling is wonderful, and I encourage it at every opportunity for parents and relatives (and me as well). I cuddle babies to feed, to talk to, to calm them when upset and to settle to sleep, but there comes a time when the baby needs to be put down, even if it is just for the parent to go to the loo, and this is where a swaddle comes in.

POSITION/LOCATION TRANSFER If you settle your baby to sleep in your arms, they are warm and secure, but when you put them down in a moses basket, for instance, they lose the security and the warmth (especially if the sheet you lay them on is cold) and they start to stir. If they are deep sleepers they may resettle themselves, but if not, they will wake again, if not straight away, then after a few minutes or when their own limbs jerk them awake.

If you swaddle them before you cuddle them to sleep, when you put them down they remain both warm and secure, just as if they were still being held. I often call a swaddle 'a portable hug', because it stays with them when you put them down so they are much more likely to remain asleep.

WHEN TO START Ideally you should start to swaddle babies from birth, as that is when they need it most, but it is possible to introduce it later. In Chapter 1 I used the example of a baby that was six weeks old who took to the swaddle immediately, and personally I would be happy to try it up to eight weeks, but not much later than that, as by that point baby is gaining strength and muscle control, and if they are used to having their arms free, may feel restricted rather than comforted.

So far I have focused on swaddles as an aid to sleep, but it also has other valuable uses:

- CALMS A BABY IN MELTDOWN whether from overtiredness, over-handling or colic. A swaddle can be an instant calming method, as not only does it provide warmth and security, it also reduces physical stimulation such as thrashing arms and legs, allowing baby to relax more quickly.

185

- **DURING A DIFFICULT FEED** When a baby gets upset during feeding, they can thrash around and upset themselves even more, in which case a quick swaddle can calm baby down enough for them to continue the feed. This is also extremely useful when feeding a reflux baby, who knows to expect pain even before they start to suck. By using a swaddle, you can get them very relaxed before you even start.

A swaddle is also an excellent way to make life easier for a new mum trying to establish breastfeeding: once swaddled, baby is much easier to hold and manoeuvre without having to deal with wriggling arms and legs. Be careful to use a very thin swaddle – if they get too warm, a new baby will stop feeding and go to sleep.

- **MAKES HANDLING EASIER** This is particularly useful when baby first arrives home. They are often passed around various family members, some of whom may not be very experienced in how to hold a baby safely. A swaddled baby is basically a secure bundle with a head (no arms or legs to worry about), so all they need to concentrate on is supporting the head, which makes it much easier on the watching parents' nerves and gives them more confidence to allow baby to be held by others.

- **REASSURANCE AND RESTRAINT** Vital for babies during medical procedures. I often swaddle babies for their vaccinations, using my favourite swaddle that can be used to restrain arms but leaves legs free. Several times this has enabled more anxious mums to feel confident enough to hold baby themselves during the process.

- **SUBSTITUTE FOR BABYWEARING PARENTS** There may be times when a baby that is used to being carried or held has to be put down, and in this situation a swaddle may help to replace temporarily the comfort they normally feel from being in a sling or parent's arms.

As with other tools, the swaddle is not a miracle cure-all, but it can be very useful, so it is worth thinking about with an open mind.

Music, sound apps, white noise

Babies can differ greatly in their noise sensitivity, depending on their temperament: while some can sleep through anything, others wake at the slightest sound, which can be very frustrating.

I have found that white noise or music can help greatly when caring for a noise-sensitive baby by masking sudden environmental sounds that may wake baby and creating a steady, predictable wall of sound around them.

When dealing with a noise-sensitive baby, the temptation is to keep them in silence while they sleep, whispering and tiptoeing around them. Not only is this inconvenient, it can create a long-term problem, as baby then becomes accustomed to the silence and cannot therefore cope with any noise at all while they sleep. I have seen this cause parents literally to become prisoners in their own home, as they daren't go out in case baby needs to sleep, and aren't able to have friends round, or play dates, or even let their other children play noisy games.

This situation is not healthy and can lead to feelings of isolation and anxiety.

MUSIC I would suggest that whatever music you choose, it should be something you and the rest of the family can hear hundreds of times without driving you insane, as you may be hearing it through the baby monitor for hours at a time. Nursery rhymes are all right for a short length of time, but not for too long. If I ever lose my mind and run amok in the future, it will be because someone has played 'The Wheels On the Bus' one too many times in my hearing!

You may also find that after a while that particular music begins to hold the same relaxing, calming associations for other family members as it does for the baby.

> I use an album called *Jazz for Babies: The Piano Album* when I am working with babies. I've heard it so many times now that I instantly start to relax whenever I hear it. It has a wonderful feel-good effect, to the extent that I put it on if I am feeling stressed with a crying baby or a difficult feed because it calms both myself and baby.

SOUND APPS There are lots of sound apps around, but bear a few things in mind when you are choosing one. Some of them have timers that turn the music off automatically, and while this can sometimes be useful, make sure you also have the option to play your app continuously as it can be heartbreaking to think baby is settling down and almost asleep only to have them wake when the sound turns off.

Sound apps work by playing a particular sample of a noise on a continuous loop, so check that there is no gap every time the loop restarts, as this can become jarring very quickly and irritating for those listening to it.

The sounds I have found to be most soothing to babies are steady white noise, rain or waves and surf noise, but there are plenty to choose from, so experiment and find which suits you and your baby.

There are also white noise gadgets such as baby toys that play sounds, or little machines aimed at adults with nature noises and rhythmic sounds to help people relax and sleep. These can be useful if you don't want to tie up your phone by using an app, but they can be both expensive and bulky if you intend to travel with them, and you really need to hear them before you buy. I keep a spare phone to use just for my baby music and apps.

The added bonus is that music and white noise will work the first time you use them, but as you continue to play them the baby will subconsciously come to associate that particular music or noise not only with sleep, but also with relaxation and the pleasurable calm that comes with falling asleep, which can be invaluable in other situations.

You can use the sleepy associations of the music or noise (along with other signals, such as a swaddle, bedtime routine, light levels, nightwear or comfort toy) to help settle a baby to sleep in unfamiliar surroundings such as on holiday or visiting family or friends, and also to help a baby adjust to travel and different time zones.

Comforters, toys

There are pros and cons to using a specific cuddly toy as a comforter, as they can help babies get off to sleep but can be a nuisance if they develop a reliance on that one toy should you ever lose it, find you have left it behind somewhere or realise as it falls apart that they are no longer being made. I tend not to use them at all with young babies, as anything in the moses basket or cot is a health hazard, but for babies over four or five months, a single comfort toy can be placed in the cot with them.

> If your baby shows a very strong reliance on a particular toy or comforter, make sure you have bought plenty of replacements for the future in case they discontinue manufacture. Bulk-buy if necessary!

A good alternative is to use something simple, such as a muslin square, but you *must* knot it so that there are only a couple of inches of loose material at either end – there have been cases of babies choking to death on unknotted muslins.

There will be times when you will need some way to distract your baby for a few minutes or longer, and toys or books can be great for this. Try to make a mental note of what sort of toys hold your baby's interest. If there are one or two in particular, it can be a good idea to put them to one side, not for daily use, so that they retain their novelty value and are more likely to catch your child's attention when distraction is called for.

Bottles and teats

These are, of course, everyday items that in some instances can become part of your toolkit.

If baby is having difficulty feeding, you may like to think about the shape of the teat and the flow rate of the bottle you are using, because in some situations either a faster- or a slower-flow teat, or a differently shaped one, may make a difference.

Babies get wind due to the inefficiency of the seal their lips make around the teat, and while some babies have no problems, others may struggle with this, sometimes due to something identifiable such as a tongue tie or cleft lip or palate. But at other times there seems to be no rhyme or reason for baby not to latch on, and it has to be put down to one of those odd things babies do.

Teats come in different sizes and shapes, so if your baby either leaks a lot of milk around the teat, or milk squirts from the sides of their mouth as they feed, you might find a different-shaped teat fits baby's mouth better.

Unfortunately there really is no way of advising which teat to try; it is down to trial and error. But I always start by noticing what shape and hardness baby is using, then try something different.

If you are using a very soft teat, try a firmer one; if you are using a teat with a very small end, then try one with a wider end; if you are using a round-ended teat, try a wider, flatter teat.

I have recently been working with a baby who regularly

squirted milk out of the sides of his mouth, so after trying various different teats (mother had a variety left over from her first baby), we found that a wide, flattened teat eliminated this problem.

Another difference between teats is the flow rate.

I would seriously suggest that all parents put water in whatever bottles they have and try drinking from them themselves, because flow rates can differ tremendously. Even though they may say they are suitable for a newborn, many teats are much too fast. This might speed up feeds, but can also lead to baby leaking, dribbling and choking, or getting frustrated because they have to keep stopping to deal with pooled milk in their mouth.

If you think the flow rate might be too fast, then experiment with other teats. This does not mean you have to buy new bottles, as many wide-neck bottles take other brands' wide teats, and likewise with narrow-neck bottles. You can always borrow from other parents who may have different bottles for you to try.

Once you have found a good teat that allows for a steady, calm feed, please bear in mind that your baby might manage better with a different teat in differing circumstances. For example, the baby I mentioned earlier got to the stage after a few weeks where he was too tired to feed properly for the last feed of the day and his sleep, which had been good, was becoming erratic at night. We changed the teat to a slightly faster flow just for that feed, and because the feed was quicker, he took the full bottle before he fell asleep and consequently slept much better.

If your baby is very upset and overwrought, you might find the opposite true and a slower flow may help to calm baby down.

There is no real way of predicting how a particular flow will affect your baby, but don't be afraid to use trial and error in an effort to find out. You won't cause any harm, and you may just stumble across something that works.

Sling, baby carrier

Most families have a sling of one sort or another, and they can be a very useful tool in a number of situations, apart from the usual one of transport.

- REFLUX Babies need to be held upright after a feed, often for fifteen to thirty minutes, which can sometimes be inconvenient for parents, so putting baby in a sling can allow them to be kept upright while freeing the parent to get on with other things.

- MELTDOWN Babies who are very upset can find the sling a comfort as they feel secure but not over-handled or stimulated as their vision is limited and sounds are muffled by the sling and the parent's body.

- WINDING Similarly, a baby who is upset and struggling to burp can often benefit from ten minutes in a sling as they are upright, which is the best position for winding, there is a slight pressure against their stomach from the parent's body, plus the movements of the parent can help dislodge wind.

Slings that hold babies upright rather than around the parent's body are better for elongating baby and helping bring up wind.

It is also a break for the parents too. More than once when I have tried every method possible to get wind from a baby and failed, I have ended up stressed and frustrated with baby still in pain. On remembering the sling, I have popped baby in, we have both calmed down, I've got on with something else, either in the house or outside, and the burp pops out of its own accord, leaving me wondering why on earth I didn't try it earlier!

Please don't worry about the type of sling you are using. There has been way too much made of the hip dysplasia possibility, but if you look closely at what hip charities and experts actually say and wade through all the sensationalist comments from social media and the press, you will realise that it is the same situation as for swaddles. Unless your baby was a breech birth, or there is a family history of hip problems, it is extremely unlikely a sling or baby carrier will do any harm, especially as we are probably not going to be carrying our babies around for any great length of time.

Choose a sling that feels right for you. Many areas have sling libraries where you can go and try on different makes and types. My only advice would be to consider how it will work for you. Make sure you can get it on and off easily by yourself. Picture yourself sleep-deprived with a screaming baby, and apply that image to buttons, zips, knots, clips. Will it annoy you to have to put it on over your head? Is it easy to adjust if it is being used by different-sized people? How much back support does it provide?

It is also important to remember that there must be adequate air flow around baby's face. In the upright slings baby just turns their head to one side, which is fine and safe, but some of the fabric slings that hold baby across your body can, if not adjusted correctly, cover baby's face. This is not safe, no matter how thin the material. A good guide is 'can I kiss my baby's face?' If you have access to do that without moving the material, then baby's face is uncovered enough.

Yoga ball, gym ball

Sometimes I go to clients and they have one of these balls left over from pregnancy or that is used for exercise, and I have found them to be very useful in stressful situations such as with a colicky baby, or when baby or parent is very upset.

If you sit on the ball and hold baby upright against your chest while supporting their head (or if they are in a sling) and bounce gently, both you and baby will find it relaxing. Baby will calm down, you will calm down, and quite often baby will burp without you having to do anything else.

> If there is no gym ball available, try bouncing on the edge of the bed instead.

You can also lay baby face down over your lap and gently roll your hips from side to side, soothing and winding baby at the same time; and you can also wind by laying baby face down on the ball and gently rolling them in different directions, but you *must* always keep one hand on your baby to prevent them rolling off.

Toolkit reminder list

This is something you may not have thought necessary, but in the heat of the moment when baby is screaming and you are stressed and exhausted it is very easy to forget some of the things that may help you, so I suggest you write yourself a reminder list.

You can do this on your phone or tablet or in baby's notebook, or anywhere around the house you can access easily. Make a note of every tool you can think of that might help, or that you have already used. These can include the equipment I have described above plus your own suggestions, and you can also record strategies or actions. For example:

What positions does my baby love or hate when happy / sad / tired / in meltdown / with wind / constipation? I've known babies that love being cuddled facing my chest when happy or with wind, but prefer facing forward if tired and grouchy.

What is the best way to distract them if upset or in pain?
• which toys work best?
• which music or song?
• dancing?
• looking out of a window?
• bright lights and shiny metal like in the bathroom?
• a walk around the garden?
• watching other children play?

Will going for a walk help baby calm down or settle? Would it help you calm down?

Which winding positions work best for baby?

Are there any situations my baby hates, e.g. loud noise, being held by strangers, being fed in a noisy room when overtired, being too hot, being made to wait for a feed?

What does my baby love? E.g. being on the changing mat, being distracted by TV/people during feeds, being naked, being under the mobile in the cot, watching trees through windows, being in a baby bouncer/chair/jumparoo, having a bath on own or with parents or siblings?

What calms *you* down, or relaxes you when *you* are stressed?
- who could you call or visit?
- how can you give yourself a treat?
- have you eaten or drunk enough?
- will a walk help?
- what music will energise you or calm you?
- are you bottling things up instead of talking about them to yourself or to someone else?
- are you being too hard on yourself?
- do you need more support from your partner/friends/family?

Remember, you are as important as your baby; perhaps more so, because they are totally reliant on you to take care of them, which you cannot do properly if you are neglecting yourself.

At the end of the day parenting is about doing your best for your baby, your family and yourself, so anything that might possibly help you is worth considering. As always, ask yourself questions, answer honestly and keep an open mind.

8.

Case studies

In this chapter I will be taking you through some of the situations I have come across while working with clients. I have tried to include those that seem to crop up most often, in the hope that they may be of some use to you both in terms of working through your own investigations and in offering possible insights and tips to try.

In some of the cases, I worked through the **AIM** process myself, and in others I involved the parents/family to differing degrees, depending on the situation and on my brief.

CASE STUDY 1

Newborn: painful breastfeeds

BRIEF First baby, girl, newborn. Parents living and working abroad, so unsure of local health and medical support. I had been booked for three months, as the parents had few friends and no family nearby, and I was there waiting when they brought baby home from the hospital.

Both parents were in favour of breastfeeding, but were not averse to occasional formula feeds for night time so I could feed and they could sleep. Eventually they wanted to use expressed milk if possible, but would not be worried if it didn't work out and they had to use formula.

Mum took well to breastfeeding with no major issues but did find it quite painful. She tried to hide it but I could see she was suffering, so I questioned dad about how she handled pain. He told me she was tough and stoic and tended to play it down, so I realised the pain was probably worse than I initially thought.

All breastfeeding is uncomfortable to start with, and some women experience a lot of pain until the baby's technique improves and the breast tissue and nipples toughen up. If the pain does not subside after a few minutes into the feed it is worth taking baby off and trying to re-latch so it hurts less. If after a couple of days the pain does not improve, it is always worth getting professional help to check the baby's latch as, if they are not getting enough breast tissue into their mouths, they end up grinding on the stem of the nipple which can be extremely painful. It can also lead to cracked and bleeding nipples, which is not only painful but can allow bacteria entry into the breast and can cause mastitis.

All breastfeeding is uncomfortable to start with

We used formula top-ups to keep baby happy until mum's milk came in, to help prevent baby biting out of hunger and frustration, but on day four there was plenty of milk. This sudden surge of milk made the breasts swollen, hard and tight but once this engorgement had calmed down, after 48 hours baby was latching well and feeding happily, just painfully for mum.

Over the years as a maternity nurse you get to know the most likely causes of problems in certain situations, 'the usual suspects' if you like, so we started thinking about those and investigating.

Our first thought was baby's latch, so we had baby checked for tongue tie then concentrated on making any adjustments we thought might help, but baby was doing a great job and nothing was wrong so we had to abandon that theory.

My next suggestion was that though there was plenty of milk, maybe the initial let-down was a bit slow and baby was getting frustrated.

With this as our next theory to test, we got mum to start hand-expressing just before the feed for a couple of minutes, then put baby to the breast. It made no difference, so we tried using the breast pump to make sure milk was flowing easily. No improvement, so we abandoned that theory too.

The next theory was that maybe the latch was good but baby herself was uncomfortable in some way, so we double-checked how mum was holding her, made sure the angle of her head was all right, along with her limbs and ears (ears often get bent back during feeding and some babies hate it). Everything seemed OK and baby fed no differently however she was held, so it wasn't that.

Could mum be uncomfortable and somehow transmitting tension to baby? Not very likely but worth investigating, so we made sure mum was comfortable with cushions. There was tension in her shoulders that was being caused by the pain of feeding, so we did our best to alleviate that with a heat pad, massages from dad, and me reminding her when I noticed her tensing. Mum felt better in herself but there was no improvement in feeding.

At a bit of a loss, I got mum some nipple shields, which made a massive difference; she was a lot happier about feeding, and began enjoying the feeds more.

At one point I noticed a drop in the amount of milk she was managing to express, which seemed to make feeds more painful, so I took her through the **AIM** process, questioning her sleep, diet, stress levels and mental and physical health and found another 'usual suspect'.

Being very fit pre-pregnancy, and wanting her figure back as soon as possible, mum, who was extremely self-disciplined, had begun cutting back on carbohydrates. They ate very healthily, and her level of carb intake was normal for her before baby was born, but she was now breastfeeding and her body had different requirements and needed those carbs. I suggested a big bowl of pasta and next day there was plenty of milk again, so we knew that she had to rethink her diet a little.

Every woman's body responds differently to breastfeeding, so balancing your diet is a very personal thing and sometimes needs a bit of trial and error before getting it right. I had one client who was super-healthy and diet-conscious and who also ate few carbs. When her milk production dropped I recommended more carbs as this usually works well, but she wasn't comfortable with that so experimented on her own. In the end, through trial and error, she discovered that all her body needed was for her to eat a small tin of oily fish a day, plus an extra handful of nuts to be able to meet the calorific demands of breastfeeding.

She was now breastfeeding and her body had different requirements and needed those carbs

My client's body appeared to respond to dietary changes, both positive and negative, extremely quickly (as did her lack of sleep and stress), which was a very useful piece of information to add to our investigations.

At one point we realised that the left breast was smaller than the right, and produced less milk (a very common occurrence due to differences in breast size and tissue and not usually a problem), so we concentrated extra feeding on the left side along with extra pumping and it did improve the flow and redress the size difference to an extent, but made no difference to the pain levels.

We reassessed the situation. We had sorted mum's milk supply, eliminated several theories and found pain relief in nipple shields, but we hadn't got to the root cause of the problem, which was frustrating.

I observed baby very carefully when she next bottle-fed to see if I could spot any clues.

I did: she was biting, hard, very hard, on the nipple at the beginning of the feed. Regardless of how hungry she was or how relaxed, she always started a feed by biting, and she bit so hard I struggled to pull the teat out of her mouth.

I had not come across this before, so began researching it on the internet. I came across lots of information about everything we had eliminated, and plenty of women complaining of severe pain, but there was never any explanation – they either just gave up or suffered.

I kept looking until finally I found an article published by the La Leche League discussing **Clampdown Bite Reflex**. They described the reflex as being present from birth, particularly in babies with strong muscle tone (baby was very strong and had a kick like a mule!), and the bite was strong enough to cut the blood supply to the nipple and cause bruising. It seemed to describe the situation perfectly, and the mum was very relieved to know that Clampdown Bite Reflex usually resolved itself after a few weeks as baby's neurological system matured.

The article suggested some practical solutions, most of which were not relevant to this particular baby, but a tip about using a finger to apply gentle downward pressure to baby's chin while feeding to counteract the clenching of the jaw improved things quite a lot. Sometimes we had to do this several times during a feed, but it did help.

Mum was very relieved to know that it would pass, and this made her feel able to bear the pain and continue breastfeeding. The bite reflex did indeed gradually fade and was gone by eight weeks, much to the mum's relief, and she went on to combination-feed successfully for many months.

Sometimes a lot of stress and anxiety can be caused by parents relying too heavily on the internet for advice, which can lead them to be affected badly by the propaganda, pressure and criticism that is rife, but in this case it proved an extremely useful source of information, especially as it came from a reliable source.

The mum was very relieved to know that there was a physical cause for her pain, and that she and others around her knew she wasn't 'being a wimp' (her words, not mine) or imagining it. I believe that even if there had been no practical solution to the problem it would still have been massively reassuring for the mum to know *what* was going on and *why*.

Mum was relieved to know that there was a physical cause for her pain, and that she and others around her knew she wasn't 'being a wimp'

CASE STUDY 2

Four days old: breastfeeding mum with low milk supply

BRIEF Baby girl four days old, first baby, mum breastfeeding but having problems.

The parents had not planned on having a maternity nurse, but hit difficulties with feeding and so called an agency I work through for emergency cover. I was booked for two weeks.

This is another example of a case where I had to solve the problem first and explain afterwards, because basically the baby was starving and mum was distraught.

As soon as I arrived I was faced with a screaming baby and terribly stressed and anxious parents.

It didn't take long for them to explain that mum had had a difficult labour and an emergency C-section and her milk had not come in. Baby was trying to latch on frantically but when she did, briefly, she was coming straight back off again and screaming. The visiting midwife had told them that they should not give any formula because baby would not then latch onto the breast because of nipple confusion; mum's breasts would not receive stimulation and so her milk would never come in. She had also told them not to use a pacifier because baby would then not suck at the breast, and that new babies could go at least seven days without milk.

I wish I could say that hearing such rubbish was unusual, but I am afraid it is quite common – and dangerous.

Every baby is different, and some sleepy babies are quite content for a few days with just the occasional mouthful of colostrum, but if your baby is screaming constantly and you have no milk, then something is seriously wrong and you have to act.

Newborn babies are driven purely by instinct, and their most powerful instinct is to feed in order to survive. This instinct has been honed over millions of years of evolution and cannot be overridden. They have no reasoning powers, and do not understand as we do that they only have to wait and food will come eventually. A new baby does not think it is hungry; it thinks it is starving. Instinct tells it that it is in danger of dying and that all it can do is scream its distress. This must *never* be ignored. You should always find a way to feed your baby, any way you can, regardless of your own feeding preferences.

Every baby is different. Some sleepy babies are quite content for a few days with the occasional mouthful of colostrum

Before I had the chance to explain this, a lactation consultant arrived, arranged by the health visitor and, not knowing the parents or the situation in any detail, I observed the session without interfering. I would like to state at this point that I know some absolutely wonderful lactation consultants that work miracles on a daily basis, but this lady was not one of them.

She worked hard at trying to help baby latch on, and there was an improvement. But she totally ignored the fact that every time she latched on, baby came off after a few sucks with no milk.

I did raise the possibility of giving some formula, but could tell she disapproved of the idea. She insisted on no bottles and gave baby 20ml from a little cup which starving baby tried to gobble and ended up choking on. I suggested a syringe as a more easily controlled way of giving milk, which we did, more successfully, but the lactation consultant insisted baby only be given a tiny amount, which had no effect on her hunger, before returning her to the breast to try again. After two hours of this she left, having instructed the parents to carry on trying baby every hour, through the night, and that she would come back again the next afternoon.

Mum was exhausted and crying, so while she tried to rest I took the still screaming baby into the nursery.

The father accompanied me and, unable to hear ourselves speak, I asked if he would mind me giving baby my finger to suck as she was desperate for comfort. He agreed and she sucked like her life depended on it, but at least we could talk.

Trying to understand the situation better, I started asking questions, and from his responses I gathered that they had suffered two miscarriages, so baby was very precious and his wife was determined to breastfeed no matter how hard it was. He wanted to support her but was not as obsessed (his word, not mine). This gave me an insight as to the mum's mindset and the cause of their anxiety.

I had noted that his wife was quite slim, and he told me she lost weight easily when stressed which, along with the C-section, went some way to explaining the delay in the arrival of milk, as her body was using its limited resources to try to heal mum at the expense of milk production.

He went to make supper while I observed baby and gave some thought as to how to proceed.

The brief of any maternity nurse is to help the parents by sharing their knowledge and experience while at the same time respecting and supporting their parenting choices, which I will always do – up to a point. Very occasionally we have to make a choice between following the parents' wishes and the welfare of the baby, and we must always act in the baby's interests.

My own research into re-admittance rates in hospitals in the UK is revealing that thousands of babies a year are being admitted for jaundice, low blood sugar and dehydration . . . all of which are closely linked to insufficient feeding and failed breastfeeding. Dehydration can cause renal failure and severe jaundice (which can result from lack of feeding), which can cause brain damage, so it is not to be taken lightly.

This baby was slightly jaundiced and still seemed alert, so I did not feel as if she was in immediate danger, but I felt I needed to tackle the subject as a matter of priority.

After supper I took baby into the parent's bedroom, where mum was resting, and we talked.

Some of what I said may seem harsh but I was careful to speak gently and calmly, without blame.

I explained that their baby was not hungry, she was starving and that every instinct in her was screaming for survival.

I explained that without milk she would soon be at risk from jaundice and dehydration, and that that would result in her being readmitted to hospital and attached to an intravenous drip and fed via a stomach tube if she was too weak to feed herself.

I gently reassured them that they had been misinformed about temporary formula feeds ruining breastfeeding and preventing the milk coming in, and that I had personally experienced hundreds of cases of temporary and combination formula-feeding which resulted in contented babies and successful breastfeeding.

The mother was terribly upset and sobbed and sobbed, haltingly explaining that she didn't know what to do, and that she felt she had completely failed by having had an emergency C-section and then not having milk. She mentioned other mothers in her group of friends from antenatal class who had all had natural births and all breastfed, and again talked about being a failure. Her husband was wonderfully supportive and said he hadn't realised she felt this badly.

I have experienced hundreds of cases of temporary and combination formula-feeding, resulting in contented babies and successful breastfeeding

I reassured her that she was not a failure in any way, and that she was a complete hero for managing to give birth at all, and that after such a shock it was no wonder her milk was slow to arrive. I gave her her baby to hold for comfort and let her cry for a while, allowing all her pain to flow out. Then, when she had calmed down, I started explaining exactly how we could help baby while protecting mum's ability to breastfeed.

I explained that nipple confusion was a myth and that with careful thought and management, it was perfectly possible to use both bottle and breast as long as we took care to ensure sufficient breast stimulation and used a very slow-flow teat to prevent baby getting lazy, leading her to prefer the easier bottle.

I pointed out that the biggest danger to mother's milk supply was exhaustion, stress and lack of food, especially as her body was trying to recover from a long labour and emergency surgery, and that the best thing she could do to help milk production was to try to relax, get as much rest as she could and eat really well.

I made it clear that baby desperately needed to feed, and that the best idea was to give her formula now and during the night while the mother rested, and that in the morning we could begin a gentle three-hourly routine of feeds with baby feeding from the breast for twenty minutes each side, then being topped up with formula so that mum's breasts were getting plenty of stimulation, baby was creating a breastfeeding habit but was then getting a full enough tummy to sleep soundly so she was refreshed for the next feed.

This was met with another flood of tears as the mother was worried that her breasts would need to be stimulated in the night. There was an element of truth in this, but my thinking was for the mother to get one really good night's sleep as she did look exhausted. However, I weighed her physical need for sleep against her emotional need for peace of mind and we compromised, with me bringing baby in to feed from her at 2.30 a.m. I would top baby up with formula if she still seemed to need it.

I felt it was important for the parents, rather than myself, to feed baby, so I prepared the slow-flow bottle I always carry with me, we dimmed the lights and they snuggled up together on the bed with mother holding baby and dad holding mum and talked them through the feed. Baby fed desperately for five minutes, then gradually started relaxing as she began to feel a full tummy for the first time in her little life. She fed well and winded easily, and after the feed I swaddled her and handed her back to her parents for cuddles and left them to enjoy their happily sleeping baby. The mother fell asleep after an hour, so dad brought baby in to me for the night.

The middle-of-the-night feed was actually quite brief as baby was still sleepy, exhausted from four days of hunger and screaming, but she did make an effort and latched on, sucking gently for a few minutes each side before falling back into a deep sleep, so didn't need a top-up.

In the morning the mum seemed better for her sleep, worried because she had given baby formula, but hopeful that we could sort it all out.

We sat down together and talked about how best to help the mother recover and relax, what foods she liked, what TV programmes she enjoyed, how much water she drank, how she felt about using an expressing machine to help stimulate her breasts and whether it was a good idea to ban all visitors so she could rest and concentrate on feeding.

We discussed how they felt about routines and demand-feeding, with me explaining all the many different options. They came to the conclusion that they liked the idea of a gentle routine but with lots of flexibility over feed times, so there was an element of demand-feeding but with structure, and we worked out a tentative schedule based on that.

I suggested we keep detailed records of feeds and allow/ encourage baby to stay latched on for as long as possible while noting the results. This way, we could use baby's behaviour as a way of monitoring any increase in the mother's milk because the more milk was available, the longer baby would stay latched. We would also note how much formula baby took, as that would help us gauge her hunger levels and give us an idea about how much we could decrease her feeds by as breastmilk increased, thus eventually weaning her off the formula.

They found this detailed plan very reassuring as it was evident we would all be working towards the goal of exclusive breastfeeding, and both parents seemed positive and relaxed.

They cancelled the second lactation consultant's visit.

We concentrated on helping the mother heal and recover, with dad cooking and bringing delicious cakes from his mother up to mum's room (she was in a lot of pain from her surgery), and all feeds were a team effort, with dad helping mum with baby and me recording times and amounts and helping with nappies and winding. Baby was completely calm and happy, eager to try the breast and feeding easily from the bottle, and on my second full day (day six for baby), we began noticing a tiny improvement in the time she fed at the breast, which was a very hopeful sign, reassuring the mother even more.

On day seven the mother's breasts started to feel tender, and on day eight her milk came in properly, leading to great celebration, despite the fact that she was in some discomfort.

We then had a difficult couple of days as mum's breasts were engorged and baby found it difficult to latch on and got quite angry about it.

At this stage we were still focusing on topping baby up with formula feeds as she struggled to latch, but once the engorgement settled down she began feeding much better from the breast. We consulted our records of her natural feeding patterns over forty-eight hours, noted how much she was taking from the bottle, then began a gradual process of reducing the formula by 5ml every other feed.

This worked well and she barely seemed to notice the decrease, and by the time I left, on day eighteen for baby, she was exclusively breastfeeding and the mother had started expressing milk after the first feed of every day so that they had some for emergencies and so that dad could eventually take over the last feed of the day. I had stressed the importance of making sure baby was always happy to feed from a bottle in case of emergencies, and so they would never have to go through the difficulties experienced by the baby and parents in Case study 3.

I had explained the **AIM** problem-solving process I used, and they had seen how it worked both in retrospect and in practice and saw the sense of it immediately. They were both open-minded and sensible and capable of asking and answering their own questions, and took to problem-solving easily. We kept in touch for two further weeks, but they had no more problems.

In this case there was an obvious starting point, but once that priority had been dealt with I could go back to the beginning, assessing what was happening, investigating why and creating a plan to solve the problem. In this sort of situation the detailed record-keeping gave us a firm basis for reducing the formula while at the same time making sure baby's needs were being met.

> *If at any time you are unsure about the advice you are being given, ask someone else, and keep asking until you get answers that feel right*

Unfortunately in this case the parents had been given bad advice, on which they stood little chance of being able to act appropriately, and baby would probably have ended up being admitted to hospital. However, the good news is that hospital admission usually results in the dehydration and jaundice being expertly addressed and remedied and parents being given proper advice and feeding help.

If at any time you are unsure about the advice you are being given, ask someone else, and keep asking until you get answers that feel right. Call another midwife or health visitor, ask to speak to your GP or call 111 for out-of-hours medical advice.

CASE STUDY 3

Three months old: difficult transition from breast to bottle

BRIEF Baby girl, three months old, exclusively breastfed. Mother going back to work in three weeks and needs baby to be able to take a bottle of expressed milk from the childminder. Baby is refusing even to try the bottle, and both mother and baby are in meltdown. I was booked for three days, twenty-four hours a day.

As you read in the case study in Chapter 1 (two-week windy baby troubleshooting job), sometimes it is easy to bring the parents into the investigation process from a very early stage, but in this case it would not have worked.

Within five minutes of arriving, I realised that both parents were extremely stressed and bickering with each other as an outlet for their emotions, and baby was beside herself with hunger, frustration and anger. What was needed was action, not words.

I took baby, gave her a pacifier and walked round the garden to distract her and managed, with much rocking and swaying, to stop her crying while mum made coffee for us all.

Just this act of being able to hand baby over to someone else was a relief for the parents, who were exhausted, and seeing baby react so positively to my handling made them feel a lot better.

They explained what had been happening, and it seemed they had done a great job for three months and that everything had gone very well, but it had all fallen apart when they tried giving bottles, as baby's reaction was instant and extreme and they had no experience of resolving such dramas.

Apparently in the first two weeks they had been in the habit of giving an occasional bottle of expressed milk, but their health visitor told them to stop because 'it would cause nipple confusion and affect milk production'!

I cannot tell you how often I have heard this, and it is infuriating because it is totally untrue and frequently leads to this sort of problem.

They tried the bottle at each feed, but sometimes they persisted and other times they gave in and resorted to breastfeeding, and every feed was a screaming battle ending in tears for everyone.

Mum had the biggest collection of bottles I have ever seen, and frequently changed bottles (sometimes mid-feed) trying to find a bottle baby would accept.

Luckily she had plenty of milk, and a good stock of her milk frozen, so at least that wasn't an issue.

The eventual plan was that once she returned to work, she would breastfeed baby in the morning, then take her to the childminder's, where baby would receive bottle feeds of expressed milk, and then breastfeed again in the evening (baby was already sleeping through the night). They had left introducing bottles so late because they had no idea it would be such a problem.

The mum admitted that she herself got very stressed and wound up very quickly and, while her partner was more easygoing, he was struggling to cope with the current situation.

I realised straight away that after four days of screaming and confusion, both parents were at their emotional limits and were in no state to listen to long explanations or face questions that would require introspection and calm thinking.

I felt that the quickest way to relieve their stress would be to begin working on solving the problem, explaining as we went along what I was doing and why and how they could repeat the process in the future.

To assess what was actually happening, I asked the mum to feed baby so I could watch, and I noticed that baby started screaming the second she was held in the feeding position, before she had even seen the bottle (so negative feeding associations had already formed). Mum was instantly stressed and physically tense, and dad was hovering, trying to help and offering suggestions, which was making the situation worse.

I took baby and calmed her again, using the pacifier, walking round the kitchen which was well lit with big windows, so nice and distracting for her.

When I touched the bottle to her lips there were a couple of seconds where her sucking instinct kicked in and she took two or three mouthfuls, then started to scream and refused to try again.

After spending twenty minutes trying several other tricks I knew, such as feeding while walking around or swaying, or in front of windows, under downlights, chatting or singing to see if I could gauge what was triggering her extreme reactions, I calmed baby with the pacifier and came up with two likely reasons for her behaviour: one environmental and the other down to temperament and emotional reaction.

My first thoughts were that the flow rate of the teats was too fast and had caused an initial upset, which was then exacerbated by baby's own temperament (which I noted was very similar to mum's) and by the parents' reactions. This had created a feeding aversion to the point where baby was so wound up she wouldn't even try the bottle. She was hungry, tired, frustrated and upset and needed help to calm down. Because she was quick to get wound up and slow to calm down, I felt that a calm atmosphere plus the use of distractions would be a good place to start.

I explained my first thoughts to the parents and how I wanted to proceed in order to test my theory.

My plan was to remain consistent and not offer any breast for the rest of the day while I continued with the bottles, but at the end of the day mum would give baby a good breastfeed to see them through the night. Baby was taking little bits of milk through the feeding attempts, and being three months old and a good healthy weight with no medical issues, I was happy that the small amounts plus a really good feed would be enough to ward off any danger of dehydration.

Having been through this scenario many times previously, I was also confident that baby would be feeding well by the end of the three days, but had to stress that this would only happen *if we remained consistent*!

I also explained that because baby had been exclusively breast-fed for three months she had formed associations that very strong-ly equated mum with breastfeeding so was experiencing confusion when the mum then tried to bottle feed. Because of this I asked if I could be the one to provide all the bottle feeds as this would lessen baby's confusion, help greatly with continuity for baby, and enable a more accurate assessment of our progress.

I then sorted through the vast collection of bottles, explaining that we needed to choose just one and stick with that, giving baby a chance to get used to it.

Teats come in different flow rates, often linked to baby's age, but there is no standard across the brands, so every make of teat for a three-month-old has a different flow rate, and the differences can be extreme.

I explained that as baby was used to breastfeeding, which is usually slower than bottle-feeding, it would be a good idea to use a very slow-flow teat, especially as she was sucking vigorously because she was hungry, which made it worse.

Luckily mum had one of my favourite bottles for this situation, which is the Munchkin Latch. It has the slowest flow I have come across, a good built in anti-colic feature and a very soft, flexible teat with a small nipple but large surround which mimics the breast very well and has yielded very good results, to the extent that I now carry one with me to all new clients.

I explained my reasoning so that the parents understood my choice and we cleared away all the others that were cluttering the work surfaces.

Mum had one of my favourite bottles for this situation, the Munchkin Latch. It has the slowest flow I have come across, a good built in anti-colic feature and a soft, flexible teat with a small nipple but large surround which mimics the breast

I explained that it would help baby's frame of mind if she was well rested before we tried feeding again, and asked what the best way to get her to sleep was. When they replied that she always slept in the pram I took her out for a walk in the park, where she slept for over an hour, while the parents tried to relax at home.

On my return I prepared the bottle, warming it slightly to mimic breastmilk, and picked her up to try feeding while she was still asleep.

Babies have a very strong instinct to suck, so one trick is to put the bottle in their mouths while they are asleep and allow their sucking instinct to kick in before their conscious brains can come up with objections. The hope is that the baby takes enough milk in the first few sucks for them to realise it tastes nice and feels good, and for their hunger to override any thoughts of protest. Basically I want them to end up thinking, 'Well, it's not what I'm used to but it isn't so bad, and I really am very hungry so I suppose it will do.'

This is what happened for twenty seconds, with her feeding calmly, then she woke up and started crying, which was disappointing, but it was a start. It meant that the flow rate was acceptable and she could cope with the teat, but that her negative feeding associations would need more work. This gave us direction for the next stage of our investigation and focused our attention on finding ways not just to overcome those negative associations, but to replace them with positive ones.

By this time it was evening, and knowing that most babies are prone to tiredness and overstimulation at this time of day, I thought about what in her environment might be adding to her stress levels, so we turned down the lights, put on some classical music and I continued feeding her while I walked round the room. Any conversation was quiet, and the whole atmosphere was a lot calmer for everyone, and we all felt the benefit.

Baby still protested, frequently coming off the teat to vent her frustrations – she really was a tough cookie! After an hour I stopped trying to feed and calmed her with a pacifier, and we took it in turns to hold her while we ate supper. She had by no means taken a full feed, but the parents said it was more than they had ever managed before, and that, plus her tiredness, helped her drift off to sleep.

The feed had been quite exhausting, and the parents were worried that it would be impossible to feed her every time walking around in dim lighting with music on, and that she would become reliant on the pacifier.

I explained that these measures were only temporary, and that once she was settled and feeding, we could gradually wean her off them. Our aim at the moment was to make feeding as easy and as pleasant as possible, and give her any aid we could to help her through this difficult period.

The last feed of the day was a breastfeed, and I helped to wind and change her, frequently waking her up so that she took a very good feed. She was so exhausted she fell asleep and slept all night.

The next morning she was already awake and hungry, so I couldn't try the sleepy-feed trick and once again it was a battle with an angry baby and me trying everything I could think of to distract her. By trial and error I worked out that the most successful solution was to calm her with the pacifier, then, when she was calm, gently slip the teat into her mouth while distracting her by walking around near the kitchen windows. In this way she latched onto the bottle several times for a few mouthfuls at a time, and we made a little progress. Again, we stopped after an hour and cuddled her between us to keep her happy until the next feed.

She had previously been on four-hourly feeds, but in this kind of scenario little and often is a good idea, so we worked on a three-hourly schedule.

The next two feeds were similar, with baby still protesting but calming down a little quicker at each feed. At about 4 p.m. I fed her the same way but added a folded muslin, so her eyes were covered to limit distractions while leaving her mouth free. She wriggled a bit but then settled to the pacifier, and this time when I slipped the teat in she accepted it and fed well for four minutes, which felt amazing!

We tried this again at the 7 p.m. feed, and she had definitely improved. The feed was still broken and she still had screaming fits, but we could see she was beginning to accept the idea.

Another late-night breastfeed followed, which not only filled up baby's tummy, but was a lovely relaxing experience for the parents, who usually snuggled down together. It was hard for them to watch their baby struggle and protest, so this was very reassuring for them.

There was a slight setback the next morning when the parents asked if they could give the morning bottle. They had watched me do all the previous feeds, so thought it would be OK.

I could tell from baby's crying that all was not well, and when I went to investigate I found that mum had tried to feed sitting in bed with none of the tricks or props I had been using. She thought that as the feeds had been improving, it was OK to feed normally, but baby was not ready for that yet.

I explained that it was way too soon to assume success, and that with a baby as sensitive as hers, with such strong objections to the bottle, we had to go at a much slower pace and invest a lot of time and effort in making sure she was happy and secure when feeding before removing the props. I totally understand this impatience as I frequently feel it myself, but I have learnt from my mistakes and now err very much on the side of caution and take my time.

I reassured mum that no harm had been done, and I calmed baby as best I could and fed her an hour later using the muslin, movement and distraction. Baby took longer to accept the bottle but did settle eventually, and had what for her at this point was an acceptable feed. It was still very on and off, with crying, but with bouts of feeding for a few minutes at a time.

A major breakthrough came when I took her for a long walk, then sat outside with her in the pram. I got the bottle ready, picked her up while she was still asleep and slipped the teat into her mouth while walking around the garden (without the muslin covering her eyes). She fed beautifully until she had taken three-quarters of her bottle, when she stopped for winding. She then refused to take more, but we were very happy with that massive improvement.

I believe this happened because we had worked on getting her well rested, comfortable and sufficiently distracted enough to allow her hunger to guide her.

The next feed was the evening feed, and she was more restless, so we used the muslin, and again she fed very well. This time, once baby was busy feeding, I stopped walking around and sat down and she continued feeding, which was another small victory.

The next morning was my last day, so mum and dad took over the feeds with me coaching and advising, and they managed to reproduce being able to get baby feeding and to sit down once she was settled, and we even progressed to having her eyes uncovered.

We sat down together and made a plan of action for them to follow once I left, including gradually removing all the props, one at a time, starting with the walking around, then the cloth and finally the pacifier. We also discussed moving her back on to her four-hourly schedule, and contingency plans for minor setbacks, for example temporarily reintroducing whichever prop they thought most appropriate for the situation, or the calmer parent taking over the feed if the other parent started getting stressed.

I emphasised the importance of record-keeping so they could accurately monitor progress and spot patterns if things were going wrong, and also that they should, as much as possible, set aside feed times to be calm and uninterrupted.

A further plan was drafted to allow the gradual introduction of other people feeding the baby, such as friends and relatives, so that she would be ready to hand over to the childminder when the time came.

I emphasised the importance of record-keeping so they could accurately monitor progress and spot patterns if things were going wrong

We kept in touch by email, and the parents continued with the plan, did a great job and by the end of the week were bottle-feeding her without any difficulty.

I have written this out in so much detail purely because it is a very common problem, and I wanted to pass on as many tips as I could and illustrate some of the traps people can fall into.

In this intense situation it is difficult to describe the investigation process in a straightforward, linear way, as I sometimes had to react with great speed, but at every stage I was assessing what was happening, trying to understand why and figuring out what to do to fix it (the essence of the **AIM** process). I came up with theories, tested them, reassessed them and then modified them, all the while trying to understand baby's and her parents' temperaments, accommodating them as best I could. I used trial and error without worrying about getting it wrong, because I know getting something wrong doesn't matter, and I trusted my instincts while drawing heavily on the parents' knowledge of their daughter.

CASE STUDY 4

Four months old: breakdown of routine, bad habits

BRIEF Second baby (boy), four months old, bottle-fed. Older brother two and a half years old. Dad at work, mum at home. Consultation over three hours.

Everything had been going well with baby on a four-hourly routine, waking once in the night, until they went on holiday. The routine became very unpredictable, plus on their return home everyone came down with a cold and baby ended up sleeping in the parents' bed for some or all of the night. The parents were very tired and struggling to sort things out while adjusting to the toddler's new nursery routine as well as baby.

I had already spoken to the baby's mum on the phone, so knew a little about the situation, which did help given the time constraints.

The parents had kept a diary up until they went away for a week's holiday (in this country, not abroad), and had then stopped as everything was getting out of control.

Looking through it, I noted that baby had been feeding well every four hours, sleeping for three good naps during the day in the pram and moses basket and had been going down to sleep at night at around 9 p.m., waking for one feed at 3 a.m. The routine had worked well as two of the daytime naps coincided with the older child's nap, giving mum time to get things done and have a break. Baby also slept well in the pram, making it possible for mum to take both children to the park in the afternoon.

During the holiday, they had let the baby's routine go in order to accommodate trips for the toddler and family meals out and, as baby was very tired, they stopped using the swaddle for baby overnight.

Two days before returning home, baby came down with a cold, caught from the older child, and to stop him from disturbing his brother they took him into bed with them at night. This continued when they arrived home, as both parents became ill and it seemed easier.

By the time everyone had recovered, the baby was used to sleeping with the parents and woke several times crying for food. He also started the day early, at around 5 a.m., and was very difficult to resettle. During the day he cried when put down, was reluctant to play by himself, cried when put down to sleep in his moses basket and his naps were much shorter. He was also fretful and unhappy.

Again, I have included this case history because it is a very common scenario. Things go along nicely, then something happens, life gets in the way and the parents find themselves reacting rather than acting, and end up doing whatever it takes just to get through each day because they are too tired and confused to sort it out.

I checked the old diary to see what routine had worked previously, and it had been very good, meeting all baby's needs. I then asked if this routine would still work now: did they want me to help reinstate that, or devise a new one?

Mum explained that her older son was going to be starting nursery three mornings a week, so would need to fit baby round that, and that she wanted to attend a baby group on one of those mornings.

Taking notes, I asked her for the drop-off and pick-up times, the baby group times (including how long it took to get there), what time the toddler woke, what time the parents woke, when they went to bed and how they divided up the childcare and household chores.

This might seem like a lot to consider, but devising a good routine is like creating a recipe for a meal, in that it can be very complex but all the ingredients must be there in order for it to work successfully.

We sat together for a while and scribbled possible timings for starting the day, travelling and meals until we had come up with the basis of a timetable.

To this we would have to add times for baby's naps, so I referred back to the diary to see how long he had been sleeping two weeks previously. It seemed that he had his longest sleep in the mornings, from 8.30 a.m. until 11.30 a.m., followed by two shorter naps of forty minutes at 2 p.m. and 4.30 p.m.

When I enquired about his current habits, it turned out that he was going back to sleep from 7 a.m. until 9.30 a.m., waking for food, then having a thirty-minute sleep at 11 a.m. and a two-and-a-half-hour sleep from 3 p.m. to 5.30 p.m., though the timings were not reliable.

I pointed out that the early sleep was probably due to baby being tired from a disturbed night, and the long afternoon nap was likely to be contributing to him not being tired enough to settle to sleep in his moses basket at night, so somehow we needed to make adjustments.

I suggested that it might be a good idea to reinstate the swaddle temporarily for all his sleeps, just to help him settle, then once everything was sorted, we could gradually wean him off it.

A swaddle is not only comforting for a baby, it also acts as a very clear 'sleep signal', in that once it is on he knows it is sleep time. The more 'sleep signals' he gets, the easier he will find it to go off to sleep, so we needed to put as many signals in place as possible. The most obvious sleep signals include where baby is placed, light levels and sound levels, as well as others such as pacifier, comfort toys, and so on. Less obvious ones can include music, radio, audiobooks, white noise, a particular scent or the feel of the cloth under their face.

A swaddle is not only comforting for a baby, it also acts as a very clear 'sleep signal' . . . once it is on, he knows it is sleep time

Baby had been sleeping all over the house, so we decided the best place would be where he slept at night, in a corner of the parents' room, but we partitioned it off by opening a wardrobe door and setting up a clothes dryer with a sheet over it because baby had become very aware of people around him and cried to be picked up when he saw anyone.

To create more sleep signals, we decided to reduce the light in the room by drawing the nearest curtain, always used dad's T-shirt as a cloth under his face as he seemed to like it, used the swaddle and chose some music. Mum suggested the radio, but I pointed out that they might have to play it during the night to reinforce the sleep message, and gentle music would be less likely to disturb her and her husband. Once she had picked the music I explained that they would both have to put baby to sleep in the same place, using the same sleep signals *every time* they wanted him to sleep.

She voiced concern that this would be impractical over time, so I explained that what we were trying to do was create a predictable and reliable sleep habit which they would use until baby was used to it. Once this had happened, they could then start to relax a little and vary where he slept, so he could sleep in the pram out on a walk or in the garden, and they could try dropping the music.

We discussed how she would handle the baby crying when put down to sleep, and after I explained some different techniques, she felt she would be happy using controlled crying, as they had used it successfully with their older child.

Controlled crying involves allowing the child to cry for short, predetermined times before going in to give quiet reassurance then leaving again. Because of his age we decided on two, three, four and then five minutes, then remain at five minutes until he settled. It is also useful to decide beforehand exactly how you are going to reassure your baby, for example, 'Good boy, mummy is here, now ssshh and go to sleep', spoken very quietly, with a gentle head stroke, then leave. If you always soothe them the same way, it becomes a reassuring and predictable mantra and really helps them settle. The night-time feed was to take place in a chair by baby's moses basket and not in the parents' bed, to maintain continuity and help him forget about the bed as an option.

Controlled crying involves allowing the child to cry for short, predetermined times before going in to give quiet reassurance then leaving again

I explained that this would be labour-intensive, so the parents had to be sure not to begin the process until both were available and had the time and patience. The mum suggested that the weekend would be a good time because the toddler could go to sleep over with her parents, which would make things a lot easier. I also stressed that once they started, they had to continue until baby was settling, otherwise they were not helping him sleep, they were just upsetting him.

At this point they would not be trying to get him to drop the middle-of-the-night feed, but to nudge him back on to a similar routine to the one he had been on before the holiday, and get him sleeping on his own again, as he had done previously.

To help baby get the message as easily as possible, they would have to be very strict on the routine so his body clock could adjust quickly for a few days. Then they could relax more and introduce flexibility, which is always useful with a busy lifestyle and other children.

I left mum with a written routine to follow with times for feeds and naps, along with the agreed sleep plan and settling techniques. I advised that they begin on their chosen day at the first feed of the day and follow it closely through the day, allowing the baby plenty of time for the sleep signals to become familiar before bedtime.

I warned them that it might be very tiring and intensive, but that if they stuck to it, the worst should be over in two days and would improve quickly after that . . . *but only if they kept going with it.*

They would keep a diary and I would be on hand to help them over the phone or by email, and we would continually reassess and modify until everything was running smoothly.

They decided to start on the Saturday morning, and it was difficult at first. They reported later that baby did not seem to mind being put back in the swaddle but got very angry when he was put down in his moses basket and left. They were aiming for a longer morning nap, but he had already had a short nap so was not very tired, but they persevered and he did eventually settle to sleep, waking several times but looking around, not crying (observed on a baby monitor with a video option).

His afternoon naps were a little better, and the feeds were no problem, but the night time was very difficult as they were in the same room with him (they had no separate nursery). At one point the mum did want to give in and bring him into bed with her, but the dad disagreed and took over the settling so she could have a break.

Because he had had a disturbed night, baby was ready for the long morning nap, and though he protested on and off for nearly twenty minutes, he then settled and slept for the whole time. The afternoon naps were also better, with baby settling after about ten minutes' complaining and, hoping to tire baby out for an easier night, I suggested they go for a long walk in the fresh air, as this often helps babies sleep.

They also gave him an extra-long bath time using a split feed (half before the bath and half after) to tire him out some more. That evening the baby settled to sleep more quickly in his moses basket and slept much more deeply and, though they did have another battle after the night feed, it only lasted ten minutes before he went to sleep, and he slept until 6.30 a.m., which they were very happy with and felt they were making good progress.

The next day was Monday and dad was at work, so mum had the toddler plus the baby, but by this time baby was getting the hang of the sleep signals and barely complained about being put down to sleep. He slept well, so she could manage both children fairly easily.

That night there was a great improvement and baby settled quickly and slept well. He did wake twice, but was settled instantly by the soothing mantra and didn't even cry.

This took the textbook three days, and worked I think because the parents were involved in the planning process from the beginning, their parenting preferences were respected and because they could see that, once in place, the new routine would benefit the whole family and so was worth the effort.

They kept good records, and after a week, when it became clear that the afternoon naps were not quite right, we were able to use the information in the diary to tweak timings a couple of times until they felt it was sorted.

After six days, they stopped using the music for the daytime naps, but kept it for the main bedtime, and a week later they dropped the swaddle for daytime naps and after another week dropped it for night time and put baby into a sleeping bag with no problems.

I made suggestions for modifications, but they did a lot of the investigating themselves by constantly questioning and reassessing what was going on, and learnt how it was perfectly possible to solve what at first seemed like, in their words, 'a big fat mess'.

CASE STUDY 5

Five months old: recognising when and how to wean

BRIEF Three-hour weaning troubleshoot. First baby (boy), five months old, bottle-fed.

Baby was in a routine and sleeping through the night but was starting to wake from 5 a.m. onward. His daytime naps were also more disturbed and he was generally more unhappy than usual. Mum was worried about sleep regression, wanting to nip it in the bud before it got worse.

Mum was calm, sensible and organised. Baby was big and bouncing, very active, rolling around the floor, very lively and interactive and absolutely loved his bottles, drinking nearly 300ml

(8oz) at every four-hourly feed, with the last feed at 7 p.m. They had recently tried reinstating a 'dream feed' at 11 p.m. to try to help him sleep but with very mixed results, as sometimes he woke up too much and was difficult to resettle.

Mum had not kept a diary, but managed to remember the last couple of days pretty well. I looked at the times and at baby's behaviour and a pattern began emerging that he was happier in the two and a half hours after his bottles but his behaviour started to deteriorate in the hour and a half leading up to the next feed. He slept more reliably straight after a feed, and really struggled to settle to sleep the nearer it got to feed time.

When you gather information then deliberately start looking for patterns in behaviour, you begin to get an idea of what might be happening. This allows you to develop theories, which you can then either research further or test to see if you are right.

Even if you knew nothing at all about weaning, you could guess from this that something was happening based around feed times, and that it might well be due to hunger.

I have seen these symptoms – this regression of sleep, disturbance of routine and deterioration of behaviour – so many times now that I know it is highly likely that the baby is hungry and ready for solid food.

When you gather information then start looking for patterns in behaviour, you begin to get an idea of what might be happening

When I mentioned this to the mum, she told me that he couldn't wean now because she was waiting until he was six months, and she wanted to do baby-led weaning.

On further questioning I learnt that she had heard or read that you had to wait until baby was six months before giving solids, and that it was better not to give puree but only give finger foods so that baby could feed himself, and that this was called baby-led weaning.

I hear these opinions being repeated all the time and, though I do understand the need in parents to try and 'do the right thing' for their baby, in following such a rigid and predetermined approach they are sometimes doing the exact opposite.

Advice about weaning has changed a lot in recent years, going from using just baby rice, to purees, to organic and home-cooked food right the way through to the current trend for solely using finger foods. The advised weaning age has gone from three months to four months, then to six months, and is now currently swinging back to between four and six months. It has also got caught up in the breastfeeding debate, where mothers are encouraged to breastfeed exclusively until six months before weaning. To add an extra layer of confusion, in the US 'weaning' means stopping breastfeeding. The resulting confusion is causing chaos and leading to problems such as this scenario.

What anyone experienced in baby care will tell you is that most babies seem to be naturally ready for weaning somewhere between four and six months. The very latest research from experts in allergies also indicates that there is a window of opportunity between four and six months where the more new foods you introduce to your baby orally during this time, the less likely they are to develop serious eczema and anaphylactic reactions when they encounter these foods in later life. Also add the fact that this period is the most common time for weaning in cultures all over the world, whether first world or developing countries, and you have the obvious answer to the question of when to start weaning your baby: somewhere between four and six months.

But when, exactly, within this period? Whenever your baby is ready. No expert can predict it, no book or friend from a baby group or Facebook group – only your baby knows, and they will tell you, if only you are willing to listen. This baby was giving the clearest signals he possibly could that he was ready for solids; they just needed to be interpreted correctly.

I gently explained this to the mum, who was quite surprised that this could be the problem and not sleep regression or anything more sinister. Once she had got used to the idea, she was relieved that it was a natural part of her baby's development and would not need extensive sleep training and so forth.

She did raise concerns that her son was not even very good at sitting up, and so would struggle with finger foods, and I had to go on to explain that having to give finger foods was also a myth.

I have met babies that absolutely love purees and feed happily like baby birds, opening their mouths for food quicker than I can spoon it in. I have also met babies who hate it, screaming when a spoon comes anywhere near their mouths, and turn feeding time into a battleground of anger and defiance, yet settle down and eat happily when given a variety of finger foods.

At every stage in this book I have tried to stress just how individual babies are from the second they are born, and that good parenting stems from respecting this. We need to do everything we can to accommodate their temperament and personal needs – which in this case meant finding out whether they liked puree, finger foods or both – and the easiest way to do this is to try them with both.

If your baby shows no sign of wanting to wean until six months, then they will probably be able to cope with finger foods, so it makes no difference whether you try those or purees – just experiment. If, however, your baby is ready for weaning at a stage where you think they might not be able to manipulate finger foods, then I would advise starting with purees. If they respond well and seem to enjoy them, then great, carry on with purees until they can manage finger foods, then try those. Baby may show a strong preference or may love both, so just go with what they want. That is what it means to be truly baby-led.

We talked all this through and the mum agreed it made sense. At one point she did ask if it was possible to delay the weaning age by giving more milk, but I explained that sometimes the baby cannot physically drink enough milk to satisfy their hunger, and that it was not just hunger we were dealing with.

The urge in a baby to wean itself onto solid food is deeply instinctive. They are not conscious of it, but somewhere inside them their body begins to signal that it needs something more, not only in quantity or calorific intake, but in nutrients. It knows it needs vitamins and minerals, different proteins and carbo-hydrates and fibre. They instinctively know they need real food and will not be satisfied until they get it.

More worry was expressed about baby also needing the good-ness from milk, so I explained that at this early stage of weaning it is not about decreasing the milk and increasing the volume of solids, but about variety. What is most important is to set up pos-itive feeding associations so that baby sees the food as fun and interesting, not as unpleasant or a battle, so we would start with tiny quantities, just a quarter of a teaspoon of something smooth and tasty to pop on baby's lower lip so that they can lick it off themselves and experience the taste on their terms. Such tiny amounts delivered in this way are less likely to cause the gag reflex to be triggered.

We discussed when might be a good time for mum to try this; when she would have the time and energy to spare so that she would not feel anxious or rushed. I also pointed out to her that it did not have to be at feed times. Most parents either feed solids after the milk or before, or after half the bottle, and all of these are good strategies, so experiment and see what works best for baby. But there is also another option.

I have had great success with offering food 'at any old time'. Literally, have the puree ready and pick a moment whenever your baby is happy or calm and pop a little on their lips. They are already in a good place emotionally, so food will automatically have positive associations. I have tried this with a baby in a bouncy chair, on my lap, in a baby walker, propped up on a sofa with cushions and in the bath. This works particularly well with stubborn or independent babies who need to wean before they can hold finger foods (a nightmare situation!), as it can prevent confrontation situations that can arise if baby learns that a high chair means the food battle.

Remember, I am not advocating trying to feed babies who are not ready for solids, but those who are showing clear signs that they *are* ready.

Quite often you will find that bigger babies take a little longer to develop upper body strength than the more wiry ones, and this was the case here, with baby struggling to sit upright so that mum felt he would be happier being fed in his bouncy chair that he loved. That and his age suggested to us both that purees would be a good place to start.

I explained that the puree would need to be very smooth, and that it would be better received if it was slightly sweet. I have found that fruits can be overpowering in their strength and sweetness, so I tend to start with sweet vegetables such as carrot, butternut squash or pumpkin.

I then asked the mum about how she thought she would react

if baby didn't like it, wanted more or started refusing, as knowing this about yourself can help you avoid some of the traps it is easy to fall into when feeding. For instance, if you are a 'feeder', i.e. you like to feed others and see a clean plate, you might be the sort who would try to feed a baby when it had had enough simply because there was food left in the bowl.

This can really annoy babies, and can press their 'stubborn button', so if this is you, and you are making the puree yourself, it is better to make only small amounts at a time for baby and freeze the leftover puree into extra-small ice cube trays, or buy the smallest container of puree you can, decant a small amount into a bowl at feed times and make sure it goes back in the fridge to be used over two or three days. Babies enjoy repetition, so are happy to eat the same thing two or three days in a row.

We talked about how the gagging reflex is quite strong in babies, and stronger in some than others, but that it was totally normal and that they would, with time and exposure to food, eventually manage to eat without triggering it.

We worked out a feeding schedule based on the family's lifestyle which involved mum introducing puree after the 11 a.m. milk feed, using one level teaspoon from a sachet of vegetable puree. Depending on how baby reacted, she could give a tiny bit or the whole spoonful over the food-tasting session, then just milk for the rest of the day.

Giving the food in the morning meant she could monitor him for the rest of the day in case he showed any sign of allergy or upset. Giving the same food for forty-eight hours would allow the baby's body time to react. This is why new foods are generally only introduced one at a time, so that if there is any sort of a reaction mum will know which food is causing it.

We talked about how baby would only be getting small amounts of food and, though she would slowly increase the amount day by day, he would not begin to feel fuller for a few days, so she would unfortunately have to put up with his disturbed routine until this happened.

To help with this, we talked over his routine to see if there was anything we could temporarily tweak to help tide them over.

The mum was waking him from his afternoon nap at 3 p.m., giving a bottle at 4 p.m. and a bath at 5.30 p.m., a bedtime bottle at 6 p.m. and putting him to bed at 7 p.m. I suggested she left him to sleep for an extra half hour, until 3.30 p.m., bringing his bottle forward so that he had it when he woke up, then do a split feed over bath time.

I was aiming to push bath time and bedtime back, and to tire him out with more play so he would go to bed later and more tired.

I suggested:

3.30 p.m. wake and bottle
6 p.m. feed, as much as he would take
6.30 p.m. bath time with lots of play
7 p.m. feed again, as much as he would take, then quiet play
   until bedtime at 8 p.m.

This fitted in with their own timings, and they felt they could cope with the later bedtime for a week or two if it meant that baby would sleep better.

We also discussed the option of giving him a little baby rice either at the last half of the feed or just before bedtime if he still wasn't any better after three days.

Not wanting to push the parents, I left the mum to talk things over with dad and suggested that if they wanted to go ahead they could start the next day and that I would support them by phone and email.

They decided they wanted to begin the weaning, so mum gave baby some butternut squash at 11 a.m. as planned the next day, and, though initially surprised, he licked his lips enthusiastically and smiled a lot. She gave him about half a teaspoon overall and it was a very nice experience for both of them.

The afternoon nap and bottle went as planned, but I got a call at 5.30 p.m. saying baby was very bad-tempered and mum didn't think she could get him through to 6 p.m. I suggested that she put a towel down on the bathroom floor, take all his clothes off and let him roll around naked. This was sufficiently novel to distract him, and he played happily until the first part of the feed at 6 p.m.

The rest of the evening worked well and he drank 85ml (3oz) more than usual and enjoyed sitting in his bouncy chair at the table chatting to the parents as they ate their supper. He was falling asleep by 7.45 p.m., so they put him to bed and he slept until 6.20 a.m. (he had been waking previously at 5.30 a.m., with night-time waking), which they were very happy with and felt that they wanted to continue.

Mum repeated the tasting game over the next three days and gradually increased the amount to a whole spoonful as baby was very enthusiastic and seemed to want more.

The nights continued to be better, and both parents felt very positive. Mum then introduced carrot, followed two days later by parsnip with the amount, led by baby's appetite, increased to four full teaspoons.

At this point mum added another puree feed just before the afternoon nap and he continued to enjoy the experience.

About halfway through the second week, when baby was on two puree feeds a day and having half a sachet at each meal, he suddenly started to sleep later in the morning. At this point I suggested that they could try putting him to bed a little earlier if they wanted more quiet evening time, but they decided that they were enjoying the supper time together as he was always in a lovely mood, so they kept bedtime as it was and enjoyed starting the day later at 7.30 a.m.

We kept in touch and everything went very well. There were a couple of hiccups when mum once tried to get him to 'finish the bowl' when he had had enough, and another time when she tried to persuade him that he really liked apple when he told her he did not and she pushed him until he got upset, but because we had discussed these sorts of mistakes, she was prepared, and managed to catch herself in time, so no negative feeding associations were made. She learnt that if he got upset for any reason, she could stop the session and distract him with a toy and end things on a good note.

At around six and a half months he suddenly got the hang of sitting up, so they moved feeds to the high chair and started giving him finger foods to play with on the tray. He enjoyed these a lot, especially as they moved feed times to coincide with their own, but he never preferred being fed to feeding himself, always happy to have both options.

9.

what is normal?

One of the most common questions I ever hear around babies is 'Is this normal?', whether it be relating to health, appearance or behaviour.

Truthfully, most of the time the answer is yes, and in my years of experience there have been very few times when I thought there might be cause for alarm.

I understand, however, that telling someone not to worry rarely helps anyone, so in this chapter I will run through the most common worries to give you the sort of real information that might just reassure or enlighten you.

Colour

Baby's skin is very reactive to blood pressure and temperature, and they can change colour surprisingly quickly and to alarming degrees, but this is totally normal.

When they cry, baby's blood pressure goes up and the skin is flushed with blood, and the harder they cry the more they change colour, the effect of which is intensified by their translucent skin. A gently crying baby may flush slightly pink but a screaming baby can turn dark red and even an alarming dark purple. This can lead parents to worry in case their baby is not breathing or getting enough oxygen, especially the first time they see it, but as soon as baby calms down and begins breathing normally again, the blood drains away and baby quickly returns to a normal colour, so don't panic.

Babies can become pinker or redder in colour if they get too warm, and go paler when they are cooler, just like us, but because of their reactive skin the differences may appear more quickly and appear quite dramatic.

They can also appear very pale when they sleep, triggering fear in inexperienced parents, who usually rush over to check that baby is still breathing, but this is also completely normal and a result of baby being deeply asleep, with slow breathing and a lower blood pressure as they relax.

I am used to the differences produced by crying and temperature but even now, after twenty-five years with newborns, I still have that awful moment of fear and go to check a sleeping baby that has turned pale, so you are not alone.

Cord

Baby's cord can look pretty disgusting, but that is how they are supposed to look. The cord beyond the body no longer has a blood supply so it withers, rots, then drops off. Baby's own skin, blood supply, immune system and the actual belly button design means that it is very difficult for infection to track back up inside baby.

It is normal for there to be whitish or greenish ooze around the base of the cord, and for there to be tiny amounts of blood, so don't worry if you see this on the inside of the nappy when you change them. It can also smell a bit unpleasant, but that is just the smell of the dead skin, so don't worry.

Once the cord has dropped off, usually somewhere between two days and three weeks, there is likely to be a bit of bleeding as some of the healthy skin around the cord is torn slightly. This stops after a couple of days, and the area starts to dry and scab over. As it heals, little bits of dried scab flake off, and if these are then wetted by baby's urine inside the nappy, it can appear as fresh blood, so do be aware of that.

There is no need to tend the cord in any way; it does it all itself, so don't try to clean or pick at it, just let it be. The only time to worry would be if you saw the baby's tummy around the new belly button becoming red and inflamed, but that is very unlikely.

I have asked other long-serving maternity nurses about their experiences, and only one in the equivalent of 300 years' worth of newborn babies had seen an infection, so relax and wait for nature to take its course.

Eyes

Very newborn babies can have puffy faces, with their eyes only visible as tightly shut slits, but don't worry, the eyes become more visible and open up as the face gets less puffy.

SQUINT Because the muscles that move the eye and hold it in position are not properly mature yet, babies can often squint, sometimes in one eye but sometimes both – also totally normal.

The squints are usually intermittent, sometimes slight but other times extreme, and are more likely to occur when a baby is tired as the muscles are weaker, and it usually only lasts a few seconds at a time. This gradually becomes less and less as baby's muscles get stronger and better at holding the eyeball in place, and has usually corrected itself by the time they are a year old. Baby's eyes will be checked by the GP at six weeks and they will make sure that baby is fixing and following. If, however, baby has a constant squint or one that is worsening from two months of age they should be seen by a doctor and referred to an ophthalmologist if needed.

STICKY EYE is very common on and off throughout baby's first year. It has a mechanical cause, not bacterial or viral, and is simply due to the tear ducts being underdeveloped. They are often narrowed and so cannot do their job of draining tears from the eyes. This is how the eye cleans itself, so tears, and sometimes a yellow sticky substance, can accumulate in the corners of the eye, sticking the lids together as it dries.

The most common myth is that breastmilk cures it because of its antibacterial properties, but it does not cure it because it is *not* an infection. Squirting breastmilk into baby's eyes will probably not do any harm, and if it makes you feel better then go ahead, but the problem will resolve itself without any intervention on our part at all. To make baby more comfortable you can gently bathe the crusty eyes with cooled, boiled water or sterile saline solution and cotton wool or gauze whenever it becomes a problem.

PINK EYE If, however, the whites of baby's eyes become red or bloodshot then this is a sign that there is an infection. If this happens, go to see your GP and they will treat it with antibiotic cream or drops. Eye infections can quickly spread to other family members, especially children, so hygiene is very important until the infection has cleared up.

Legs, arms and feet

Babies have **bow legs**. That is just the way they are born, probably as a result of having soft bones and being curled up as they develop in the womb. These gradually straighten out over the next two years as the child starts to bear weight and to walk.

ARMS also sometimes appear short (they grow later) and curved for the same reasons.

FEET Babies are frequently born with their feet turned inward towards each other, which is known as Positional Talipes. The degree to which they are turned in can vary from slight, which is considered normal and self-correcting over two to three months, to more extreme. It is caused by pressure on the feet in the womb which leads to stiff ankles, and is not a bone defect. The condition is very common, and if necessary can be corrected by massage and exercises which resolve the issue more speedily, but does not normally cause any problems with walking later on. If the condition does not improve within two months it is a good idea to have baby seen by a doctor as further help with treatment can be given.

Strange noises

Some babies are very quiet, and you barely even know they are there, especially when sleeping, but others can make you wonder if you are sleeping in a farmyard! This is totally normal and is just a character quirk of your particular baby.

Some of the noises can be lovely, as they coo or giggle in their sleep, but others can be more surprising, annoying or even worrying.

Wheezes, snuffles, grunts, squeaks, whistles, croaks and sighs are all normal noises for a healthy baby to make and can be due to their physiology, their position and to mucus at the back of the throat or nose. Babies are also frequently sick through their noses and sometimes bits of milk can lodge in the back of the nasal passages. These gradually get dislodged or broken down but can in the meantime cause rattling or snuffling sounds at the back of the throat. As long as the noises are occasional or quiet there is no need to worry, but if the noises are constant or excessive, disturb or upset baby, or if nasal vomiting is frequent, it is worth getting baby checked by a doctor as it may be a symptom of reflux or Cow's Milk Protein Allergy (CMPA).

Crying

A lot of babies begin life with a gentle, plaintive sort of cry (designed by nature to tug at your heartstrings), but some babies are born with their volume switch set to maximum and come out screaming at the top of their lungs, which can be quite a shock.

After a few days of interacting with your baby, you will begin to get to know their own particular cry and will later learn what each different cry is expressing, and you will also learn what is normal for your baby.

At the beginning you might find the crying alarming and confusing and wonder how you will ever figure out what is wrong, but it will come with time, don't worry.

It is not only the frequency of your baby's cry that is unique; it is also the intensity. I have come across babies that cry gently, while others shriek like a steam train whistle, and yet others that have great throaty, blood-curdling screams that are extremely alarming for anyone who does not know that particular baby. All types of cry are completely normal.

SCREAMING Sometimes when a baby is in full scream, they will exhale until you can see their lungs are completely empty and then there can be a slight pause of a few seconds before they breathe in again.

The first time you witness this it can be terrifying, especially as baby is often bright red or purple in the face at the time, but again, this is normal and they will breathe in again when their body tells them to. If you are worried, try picking your baby up and interrupting the scream by somehow distracting them with movement or with a noise or handclap, or call their name loudly.

Once you know your baby's temperament and habits, any changes in frequency or duration of their crying can give you clues as to any problem such as discomfort, pain or illness (a baby with meningitis has a very distinct, inconsolable high-pitched wail/scream, for example, which might alert you to the need for further symptom checks), so it is worth spending time getting to know your baby's own normal range of cries.

Head shape

The heads of newborns can vary tremendously depending on how they were lying in the womb, and also on what sort of birth they had.

The more intervention they experience, the more chance there is that baby's head will be misshapen to varying degrees, for instance with a forceps or ventouse delivery, they may have large lumps and bruises on their head, or have a very pointed head. This, while distressing, is still classed as normal for that situation and resolves itself gradually over time.

FLATHEAD There is a lot of talk about 'flathead' being a problem, but most of the time there is absolutely nothing to worry about.

The problem is said to stem from the fact that we now put babies to sleep on their back and not on their front, so, depending on the way their head lies on the cot mattress, baby may have an area around the sides or back of their head that is a little flatter than the rest, but this is also normal.

If your baby was born with the same tough skull that we adults have, their heads would risk being cracked during birth, as would the mother's pelvis. To allow nature to take its course, therefore, their skull is made up of soft plates that 'float', and by that I mean they are not joined together. The most obvious place to observe this is the fontanelle at the front of the top of baby's head. The soft bony plates do not meet, and there is what can sometimes be an alarmingly large gap where the brain is protected by nothing more than fluid, membrane and skin (also totally normal).

The fact that these plates are soft and not joined means that there is quite a lot of opportunity for them to move and, if repeatedly placed in the same position, for the head to become slightly mis-shapen. However, worrying though this is, it usually resolves itself by the time baby is one year old. There are various special pillows and gadgets such as helmets available that promise to correct an irregular-shaped head, but there is little evidence that they work.

The simplest, cheapest and most effective solution is to vary the position of baby's head when they sleep. Even if you put your baby flat on their back, their head will naturally tilt slightly to one side or the other, sometimes as a reaction to light, or to a rise in the floor, a tilt to a moses basket or toys on one side. All you need to do is gently move baby's head to the opposite side for some of their sleeps. However you remind yourself to do this is down to you, but I tend to tilt baby's head one way for daytime naps and the other for night time, or just change every few days whenever I remember.

People also suggest tummy time as an antidote, but babies under three months are rarely happy on their tummies for more than a few minutes at a time, and such a short period is far too brief to make any difference at all to head shape.

Having spoken to different paediatricians, most of the parents that are referred to them for cases of 'flathead' have absolutely no cause for concern and are sent away with the instruction to come back at nine months if baby is not better after basic position changes.

As adults, very few of us have perfectly shaped, smooth skulls; we have lumps and bumps and flat bits, but most of us never give it a moment's thought because our head is covered by hair. A baby's head, by comparison, has little or no hair, and so every tiny imperfection is visible all the time, giving worried parents something else to fret about. As baby grows, their head will even out and their hair will grow and cover any remaining bumps.

If you are still worried or have any doubts, however, always go and see your GP, or mention it to your midwife or health visitor to allay your fears. Never leave any question unasked that may give you reassurance and peace of mind.

Appetite

Babies' appetites are not just unique to them, but can change from day to day, hour to hour for no apparent reason, leaving you wondering what on earth is going on.

Where appetite is concerned, I would advise you to go with the flow. Over the days and weeks, as you and your baby become more proficient at feeding, you will get to know what is normal for your particular baby.

Do be aware, though, that babies are often not consistent in how long they feed for or how much they take.

I frequently hear parents worrying that baby had a certain amount at every feed yesterday, but is only taking half that today, and wondering what is wrong. Baby's appetites can be affected by how tired they are, how thirsty or hungry they are, how hot or cold they are, what mood they are in and how active they have been, exactly like older children and adults, so if you are worried by a change in feeding habits, go back to being a detective and think about what might be causing it.

I know the instinct to feed a baby is very strong and parents, especially new ones, tend to use it as a guide to how well they are doing, but healthy babies are very good at taking the food they need, when they need it. They also tend to even things out over twenty-four or forty-eight hours, so as long as there are no other symptoms and baby seems well in themselves, try looking at the amounts taken over a longer period. If however you notice a rash, abnormal sleepiness, fever or inconsolable crying, dry nappies, or the behaviour continues over several feeds (especially if baby is under two months old) then get baby checked by a doctor.

LACK OF APPETITE This can be a sign that your child is fighting off some sort of bug or illness, so keep an eye on the rest of their behaviour over forty-eight hours, which is the usual incubation period for most common illnesses such as colds.

INCREASED APPETITE Baby's appetite can also increase when they are having a growth spurt. They seem to eat more than usual for two or three days, then sleep more than usual and, though some people doubt it really happens, I have seen it far too many times to be in any doubt.

Quite often we only notice the growth spurt when baby suddenly seems to be sleepier than usual and the parents worry that they are ill. In this sort of situation, I always encourage parents to look back either in the diary or in their minds to see what's happened in the last few hours or days. Did something happen that might account for the current situation? Clues to look for in this case involve changes in appetite, which can sometimes be an increase in amount taken, but can also be how hungry they are just before the feed. They may not take more milk, but may seem ravenous when they start feeding.

It is often quoted that growth spurts take place at three weeks, then at particular set times. Though I have noticed the first growth spurt take place at around two to three weeks, I have found that after that, babies seem to experience them at different times, so do not be worried if your baby's growth spurts don't match a particular book or website's predictions.

Wind

I have gone into winding in quite a lot of depth in Chapter 6, but what I need you to know is that regardless of how much wind your baby takes in when they feed, how easily that wind comes up and whether it comes in a few big, noisy burps or many tiny, silent ones, all of these aspects are unique to your baby. You may be able to help reduce the amount of wind your baby takes in by adjusting bottles or latch, but the rest you will need to adapt to dealing with.

As a vast generalisation, babies do one or two big burps when you first start winding them, then often have a few more small ones as you continue, but it is always worth winding for a few extra minutes if you are not sure your baby has finished.

It is totally normal for some babies to be extremely windy and others hardly at all. Some very lucky parents have a baby that needs little or no winding, though that is rare.

It is normal for babies to bring up some milk when they burp, either a small amount or quite a lot. One of the misconceptions is that if your baby is sick a lot they must have reflux, but that is not true. If your baby is perfectly happy, with no discomfort or any other reflux symptoms, it could just be that you have a sicky baby. If you do, there is nothing much you can do about it, apart from winding them upright and quite gently and passively, and using lots of bibs and muslins while you wait for them to grow out of it.

Hiccups

It is totally normal for babies to get hiccups either when they feed or just before or after they feed. Some babies hardly get any, but others get them all the time, and it is often said to be linked to how much the baby hiccuped in utero, but over the years I have come to realise this is a myth and that the amount of hiccups a baby gets is purely down to their own physiology and the amount of wind they take in.

The hiccup is caused by the baby's diaphragm contracting sharply in response either to wind trapped in the stomach or to wind that has just come up, and is more frequent in babies because they take in more wind when they feed, have not learnt how to burp for themselves and have an immature digestive system. Gradually their bodies get used to dealing with wind and the hiccups become much less frequent.

Some babies barely notice the hiccups, but it is also normal for other babies to get quite upset by them. If you need to speed things up so you can finish the feed or settle baby, you can try and get rid of the hiccups by either letting baby cry briefly (a few seconds is usually enough), helping them fall asleep, giving them a pacifier to suck or giving them something to drink (milk, water, gripe water). I have also found that a drop of Infacol (simethicone) can sometimes help.

Breathing and temperature

Both of these things can cause a lot of worry for new parents, so I have put together the norms for easy reference.

It is very easy to become worried when you first see your baby breathing rapidly, but this is normal for them as their breathing rate is **30 to 60 breaths per minute (0 to six months, at rest)**, whereas for adults it is 12 to 20 breaths per minute, which is a big difference.

It is also normal for baby's breathing to be shallow, irregular and to involve grunts and other noises. If your child seems happy and healthy and behaving normally, then don't worry.

If they seem sleepy or fretful and have a temperature, then keep an eye on it. If breathing goes **over 60 to 70 breaths per minute**, seems laboured, or if you can see the skin just above the centre of the collarbone at the base of the neck going in and out at each breath, then speak to a medical professional.

TEMPERATURE Our own temperature varies from 36.1°C (97°F) to 37.2°C (99°F), depending on our own personal norm, as well as on our health, activity and environmental factors.

A baby's normal temperature is about **36.4°C (97.5°F)**, but that can vary from baby to baby, so it is always a good idea to get to know what is normal for your particular baby by taking their temperature several times over two days, at different times of the day. This will give you a range of averages to refer to, and will also ensure that you are familiar and competent with whichever thermometer you are using.

FEVER Generally a fever is anything over **38°C (101°F) if baby is 0 to three months**, but a *persistent* temperature of **37.5°C (99.5°F)** in a baby **under 2 months** should be investigated medically as soon as possible, and over **39°C (102°F) if baby is three to six months**, and is the temperature at which it would be advisable to seek medical help.

Be aware that your baby will feel hotter if they are or have been crying, have had a bath, are in too many layers of clothing or have been over-swaddled/-wrapped in too many blankets, so if you think this may be the case then wait, unwrap them and calm them down for a few minutes (assuming they seem healthy in other ways) and then recheck their temperature.

FEBRILE CONVULSION Babies over six months old may experience a fit or seizure known as a febrile convulsion as a result of a rapid and sudden rise in temperature (often due to an infection or virus). If you notice such a temperature change you may be able to prevent a febrile convulsion by cooling baby down, so strip them off and use a fan and try and reduce the temperature. If they do have a seizure, place them in the recovery position and call an ambulance and get them checked out, though there are usually no lasting effects. .

Sleep

A very new baby may sleep deeply for hours at a time, or wake frequently and seem hardly to sleep at all. Both can be considered normal, but it is more usual for a well-fed, well-winded baby to sleep for longer periods, so if your baby is waking frequently or doesn't sleep much, it would be a good idea to work through the investigation process described in Chapter 4 to eliminate any problems.

Once you are sure you are feeding and winding well, and your baby settles into some sort of pattern or routine, you will begin to get to know your own baby's sleep patterns and preferences.

Some babies sleep very soundly, oblivious to all noise, while others are light sleepers and can be woken by the slightest sound.

Some babies sleep very deeply, lying very still for hours at a time, which can be a little alarming for new parents, but if you are worried, go over and check that they are all right. I usually gently touch their chest or head and watch as they stir to reassure me. Other babies are wrigglers, and move around or make all sorts of strange noises, which is also normal and less worrying. Sometimes these wriggling sessions are due to the baby coming up out of a deep part of their sleep cycle into a lighter one, or from digestive discomfort.

A lot of the time they will just drift off back into a deeper sleep again, but parents can frequently misinterpret the stirring as signs that baby is waking up for a feed and pick them up, waking them unnecessarily, so it is always worth waiting a few minutes to see if they will resettle, or trying to soothe them gently back to sleep if you think they are still tired.

You may find that there is a pattern to when your baby sleeps the deepest or the longest; for instance, most babies will sleep more deeply for either the first or the second half of the night, and more lightly for the other half, or they may prefer to have their longest nap of the day either in the morning or the afternoon. This is a very useful pattern to notice, as it can help you when setting up or altering a routine, or planning your day.

Birthmarks

Birthmarks in babies are extremely common, and most will fade within the first year.

STORK MARKS OR SALMON PATCHES These are pink or red patches that appear at birth, usually on the eyelids, forehead and the back of the neck, but can be anywhere. They are flat (not raised) and are caused by abnormal blood vessels under the skin and usually fade within a few months, though those around the back of the head and neck can take up to four years to fade.

STRAWBERRY BIRTHMARKS (HAEMANGIOMA) These are raised patches of red skin that can appear anywhere on the body. They increase in size for the first six months, then begin to shrink. It can take up to seven years for them to fade completely, but are usually left untreated unless they are somewhere that may rub and therefore bleed, or are interfering with the eyes or with feeding.

MONGOLIAN SPOTS These are most common in dark-skinned people and are usually found over the buttocks and lower back, but can also be found elsewhere. They can be small or quite large but are harmless and don't need treatment, though they can take two to three years to fade.

All of these birthmarks are very common and affect over 50 per cent of babies, and are self-resolving.

PORT WINE STAIN A very small number of babies are affected by the more permanent birthmark called a port wine stain. If your baby has one of these it is easy to recognise because of the flat, dark purple stain-like appearance of the mark. These can be tiny but can be large, usually affecting the face and back. It is a permanent mark but will be obvious from birth, so will be explained and addressed in hospital or by your midwife at a home delivery.

WEIRD LITTLE FUNNY BITS You will also come across what I describe as 'weird little funny bits', i.e. spots, blobs, blotches, stripes, patches and lumps, which seem to appear then disappear before you get a chance to identify them properly. That is also normal and nothing to worry about.

Urine, faeces and constipation

URINE Baby's urine is normally clear or light yellow with only a slight smell, but as the urine gets more concentrated it becomes darker and stronger-smelling. This usually happens during the first four or five days of their lives if breastfeeding, because the milk doesn't come in immediately so baby is not taking in much fluid. This is fairly common, and as long as the nappies are wet there is nothing to worry about and should soon improve as mother's milk arrives.

> Putting a thin cotton wool pad in the nappy where you would expect the urine to go will make it easier to see, as nappies draw urine in so it's harder to spot.

During the first twenty-four hours it is also possible that you may see orange, red or pink powdery stains in the nappy (known as brick dust). This is due to urate crystals, which are caused by the concentrated urine. It can be a bit worrying when you first see it, but it usually passes when the milk comes in and the urine becomes more dilute. However, if you are exclusively breastfeeding and the brick dust remains, is present in several nappies, or gets worse, it could be a sign that your baby is at risk of dehydration so get your baby seen by a medical professional as soon as possible.

Occasionally I have come across babies who quite naturally have very strong-smelling urine, even when very dilute, which can smell so strong you would think the nappy was dirty. As long as they are healthy in every other way, it is just something you will get used to over time.

Once your milk has come in, or once baby is on formula, it is all right to see occasional dark-coloured, concentrated urine, but if there are several dark, wet nappies a day it is better to have it checked by a doctor.

Once feeding is established, your baby may pass urine twenty times a day, which is totally normal, but you do not have to change them every time, especially if they are asleep. A nappy change at feed times is perfectly adequate.

MENSTRUAL BLOOD This can sometimes be seen as a faint pink stain, or a much darker stain in the nappies of baby girls, and is due to pseudomenstruation. It is exactly what you would expect from the term: false menstruation brought on by the massive flux of hormones around the mother's body and passed through the breastmilk. It is temporary, lasting a few days, and stops once the mother's hormones begin to settle. I have seen parents get very upset by this, but it really is very common.

Babies, both boys and girls, can also get hard and swollen nipples for the same reason, occasionally even producing a little colostrum when gently squeezed. Don't panic. It is perfectly natural, and passes very quickly.

Once feeding and hormones have settled down, usually after a couple of weeks, if you see blood in baby's nappy get it checked out by a doctor, but also remember that if mother is breastfeeding and has cracked, bleeding nipples, there may be undigested dark-coloured flecks of blood in baby's faeces.

FAECES Most parents are warned beforehand about meconium poo, but even so it can still be a bit of a shock when you first encounter it.

When your baby is in the womb, they are ingesting all sorts of material including skin cells, mucus, amniotic fluid, lanugo (fine hair), bile, and so on. Once baby begins to feed, whether on colostrum or formula, this material begins to be expelled from the body. It is a thick, sticky, black or dark green tar-like substance which sticks like glue to baby's bottom and can be hard to remove.

Don't bother trying to remove meconium with cotton wool balls – it is impossible. Use either flat cotton wool pads or, even better, a wet wipe, followed by cotton wool and water if you are worried about chemical residue.

Moving on from sticky tar, the next 'poo stage' looks like wholegrain mustard. Once baby is drinking milk rather than colostrum, the digested milk shows in the faeces as flecks of yellow, which gradually become more numerous until the whole stool is yellowish and lumpy.

In a breastfed baby, poo is usually fairly liquid and can have lumps within a watery stool, while combination- or formula-fed babies generally have a thicker poo texture. The more formula they have, the thicker the poo is, sometimes coming out like toothpaste from a tube.

Sometimes there are pockets of wind that come out with the faeces which, if you happen to be changing baby when they poo, can make things interesting because the poo becomes jet-propelled. It can come out in small splats, or it can be expelled like a rocket and travel several feet, so be warned! This is called projectile poo and seems to be just a peculiarity of that particular baby rather than something wrong or changeable.

> *Always* have the clean nappy open and ready to go *before* you remove the old one, and get it in place as quickly as you can. If you hesitate or forget, you may regret it!

Sometimes the faeces of a breastfed baby may become more green, foul-smelling and gassy. This is very common and nothing to worry about; it is most likely caused by baby taking in too much of the thinner foremilk and not enough of the thicker hindmilk. If you think this may be happening, make sure baby is draining one full breast before offering the second.

Sometimes you may see flecks of dark brown blood which, when wet, may leave a pink stain. This is caused by blood from cracked and bleeding nipples being partially digested by baby and is nothing to worry about.

If you see fresh blood, or blood that looks like redcurrant jelly, it could be a sign of internal problems, so contact your doctor or NHS 111 immediately.

CONSTIPATION It is very common for babies to become constipated and is not serious, but may make baby uncomfortable.

Constipation can be caused by baby getting dehydrated, either in hot weather or by not drinking enough milk, where the body takes back water from the faeces in the intestine to use elsewhere in the body. The stools then become harder and more difficult for the body to expel. The most effective way to help this is to give baby a small amount of sugar water, which will encourage water back into the intestines, making the faeces softer and easier to expel.

Constipation can also be caused by a sudden increase in the amount of formula a baby drinks, as it can take their bodies a few days to adapt to the increase in waste products it has to deal with. If possible, try to increase formula intake gradually, but if this is not possible just have sugar water on hand. It may be that baby has slightly harder faeces for a few days, but if they stop having dirty nappies or seem uncomfortable in any way, then use the sugar water.

> For a constipated baby, use ½ teaspoon of sugar dissolved in 30ml (1oz) boiled, cooled water given by bottle.

Every baby is different in terms of how many dirty nappies they produce in a day. They may poo at every feed, or once or twice a day, or even every other day. Breastfed babies in particular can go several days between poos because there is less waste for the body to deal with and every last scrap is being used. Keep a record of dirty nappies and use it to get to know your own baby's pattern, and don't worry if it differs from examples in books or medical information.

> All the statistics and guidelines you see relating to how much babies pee, poo, drink and weigh are averages, and only give a rough idea at best. Just learn what is normal for your own baby and, as long as they are happy and healthy, stop worrying.

Skin rashes

This will be your baby's favourite way to make you worry, as they seem to be able to come up with unidentifiable, mysterious rashes at the drop of a hat!

MILK SPOTS The first rash you usually encounter is the milk spot rash. Contrary to its name, it has nothing to do with milk or how you are feeding and is equally common in breastfed and formula-fed babies.

Somewhere in the first month you will begin to notice small white pimples under baby's skin around their nose, which are hardly noticeable at all. They also usually get slightly larger, raised red pimples, more like adult spots, and these can come up for a few days and then disappear again anywhere on their body, but usually on the face and sometimes the nappy area.

Some babies just get one or two spots here and there, while others can suffer badly, seemingly covered in an alarming red rash which can cover their whole face. This can be very distressing for parents, and I am often asked what they can do to get rid of them, but the advice I always give is to do nothing.

Nobody knows exactly why the spots occur, but the most popular opinion is that it is due to baby's immature oil glands functioning inefficiently. The skin is not infected, just unsightly, and tempting though I know it is, please resist the urge to 'do something' to help.

No squeezing, lotions, liquids, creams or scrubs will help in any way, and some can actually cause lasting damage. I had one mum who used a blackhead-removing adhesive patch on her son's nose, and instead of baby having insignificant white pimples, he ended up with a nose covered in red and bleeding pores which looked very obvious and took weeks to heal. Babies are excellent at self-healing in the first few months, so it is better to let them get on with it, and they will very quickly end up with the perfectly balanced skin we associate with babies.

CRADLE CAP While not strictly a rash, I have included cradle cap here because we are dealing with skin issues.

As with milk spots, we don't know the exact cause of cradle cap but it is most likely a combination of overactive oil glands in the scalp and unremoved dead skin. It can appear as a flaky scalp, or as patches of white, slightly thicker scales, or as thick, yellowish patches, depending on how long it has had time to build up.

It is not, at this point, an infection and does not need harsh shampoos or chemicals; in fact, these are likely to strip the scalp's natural oils and stimulate the production of even more oil, exacerbating the situation.

Preventing cradle cap is very easy, by exfoliating baby's scalp with a soft baby hairbrush as part of their daily routine. This stops the dead skin sticking to the oil being produced.

If it does start to build up, the best way to remove it is by soaking the area with a mild oil such as almond or coconut for an hour, then, either in the bath or holding baby over the sink, using the soft baby hairbrush to rub round and round, physically removing the softened skin. Frequently dip the brush in warm water and repeat, and, if necessary, use the tiniest drop of the mildest shampoo you can find (remember, we are trying not to stimulate more oil production by stripping away the natural oils) on the brush to help break down the oils that are holding the skin to the scalp. If you do this slowly but firmly, your baby may even enjoy the experience, as it will feel like a massage.

If the cradle cap is extensive or very thick, don't try to remove it all in one go – do it gradually over a few days until it has gone, then make sure you brush their scalp every day with a dry baby hairbrush.

In some cases, where the cradle cap has either been left a long time or has been picked at by overly zealous adults, the skin can become infected by bacteria and yeast, in which case it is a good idea to have it checked by a doctor who will probably suggest a medicated shampoo.

SWEAT RASH This is caused by skin being left damp for long periods of time, causing an irritation. Quite often this happens in older babies as they get folds of fat, so just be sure to check and clean (with cotton wool and water) in the folds around the neck, the armpits and the thighs, then pat them dry. It can also occur in the area under the bib if baby is sick or drools a lot. All you can do in this case is make sure the area is kept clean, and use extra or plastic-backed bibs. If it does look sore or baby seems irritated, then use a very thin layer of Sudocrem overnight, then go back to trying to keep the area clean and dry during the day.

ECZEMA This shows as dry, itchy, red and cracked skin, usually around the face and neck and in areas of creased skin such as wrists, elbows and the backs of knees. A predisposition for eczema can be inherited, so if either parent is prone to allergies, eczema or hay fever, then be on the lookout and have any suspicious dry patches checked by your doctor as soon as possible.

FLAKING SKIN Sometime in the first two weeks of life your baby will naturally lose the top layer of skin which has done its job of getting baby from being aquatic to being a land mammal and is no longer needed. Baby's skin will start to flake around creases such as at the ankles and wrists, and will spread over the whole body, including the face.

This is totally normal and is *not* dry skin. I constantly hear people say that baby has dry skin and has to be oiled, but that is totally unnecessary. The skin will come off whether you oil it or not, and applying oil will slow the process, sticking the skin back down when it is trying to come off. While oiling generally does no harm in itself (as long as you use a very mild oil – not olive oil, which is too harsh), it can lead to parents using detergents to bathe baby to get rid of the oil, which in turn leads to the skin drying out or reacting to the chemicals, which requires more oil and creates a vicious circle. A baby's skin is perfect, and naturally capable of balancing itself without any help from us, if we give it a chance.

I began recommending that parents use no chemicals whatsoever on their babies when there was eczema and allergies in the family, as a precaution, and found the babies had such perfect, healthy skin that I now advise the same for all parents. I know it is tempting to use one of the many beautifully scented and packaged bath products on your baby, or essential oils, especially as they promise to be natural or organic, but the truth is that even the gentlest of these is still too harsh for new baby skin and will just strip their natural oils and dry them out. Apart from the very occasional drop of very mild shampoo for cradle cap, there is no need to use anything except water on your baby for the first six months.

NAPPY RASH This occurs when faeces and urine react together and damage the top layer of skin around baby's bottom, causing a red rash and blisters.

This can happen very quickly in babies with sensitive skin, so parents should not feel guilty if it happens. There are a large number of creams all claiming to be soothing and healing, and it can be very difficult to know where to begin, but, having tried pretty much every possible cream over the years, I have come to the conclusion that less is more, and simple is better.

Babies have amazing skin that heals itself very quickly if conditions are right. This means they don't actually need help to heal – we just have to figure out how to create the optimum conditions to *allow* them to heal.

We know what caused the problem in the first place, so all that is needed is for there to be a barrier between the healing skin and the damaging urine and faeces, and I find a simple barrier cream is perfectly adequate for the job. My favourite is Sudocrem, because it sticks to the skin and protects it for a long time and is also gentle but soothing, with few ingredients. I clean the affected area with water, pat it dry (with the clean nappy, as this leaves no fibres behind like cotton wool) and then add a thick layer of Sudocrem to protect the area for as long as possible.

Change the nappy more frequently than usual, and immediately you suspect a dirty nappy. Whenever you can, give baby a few minutes of nappy-free time to let air circulate and help dry the skin off. This usually shows an improvement overnight, and solves the problem within a few days.

If baby poos frequently or the nappy rash is persistent, I switch to using Lansinoh lanolin nipple cream, as it is by far the best barrier cream there is: it stays on for ages and works very well.

THRUSH This is caused by a fungal infection of the skin which is normally associated with a vaginal birth, but which can affect any baby, boy or girl, at any time.

It begins like nappy rash but does not respond to the usual nappy rash treatment, instead spreading rapidly and causing bright red, raised patches all around the nappy area. If left un-treated, thrush can very quickly cause blistering and bleeding.

If you can get a doctor's appointment quickly, then do so, but if not, then go to your pharmacy and get one per cent Clotrima-zole cream. This is the same cream as we women use on our own outbreaks of thrush, but is weaker. Some brands may be labelled as nappy cream, but others just as one per cent.

Clean the affected area, dry it, apply a *thin* layer of cream (more is *not* better) no more than twice a day, as the cream can be harsh if overused, and then leave baby with nappy off for a few minutes to allow the cream to dry a little so it doesn't rub straight off on the nappy. Then put the nappy back on.

Do not apply any other cream on top to protect from urine and faeces, because this will create a warm, damp environment which is exactly what the fungus needs to multiply. Change the nappy as frequently as you can, and leave baby's nappy off as much as possible to allow the skin to dry out.

MYSTERY RASH Sometimes, despite all our experience and our frenzied internet searches, babies can still suddenly appear with a mystery rash that is unidentifiable and leaves us worrying about what it might be. This will happen at some point, and all you can do is assess your baby's overall general health and behaviour and keep an eye on it. Keep a record of when you first noticed it, and if it changes or progresses in any way.

The great majority of the time whatever it is will resolve itself, and the best thing you can do is leave it alone, but if at any point you are worried, then go and see your doctor and take along any notes you have made which could help them with a diagnosis.

10.

Where and how to get help when you need it

Sometimes, no matter how hard you try, there will come a time when you need to ask someone for help or support. That is not a sign of failure, weakness or bad parenting; it is simply that the problem is beyond your experience or expertise.

I have twenty-five years' experience, and I readily admit that I sometimes need help from medical and other professionals because no one can be an expert in every field, no matter how many years' training they have; it is not humanly possible.

Even if you decide you need some sort of help, it can be very confusing as to where to go or who to ask, because you may not even know what the problem really is.

This chapter is aimed at explaining the help available and guiding you through the possibilities, along with tips to help you get what you need.

But before I go any further, I want to address the subject of receiving poor help or bad advice.

Other people's opinions

One of the main reasons I wrote this book is because of the current parenting context, whereby everybody not only seems to have their own opinion about the best way to parent, but also feels it necessary to force their opinions on other people. This, I'm afraid, is no less prevalent among healthcare and other professionals, so you need to be ready to deal with this and either redirect your request for help to another person, or refocus the request with regard to your specific need.

For instance, you may ask your midwife for advice on combination feeding, only to receive a patronising lecture on the benefits of exclusive breastfeeding. At best this is totally unhelpful, and at worst can trigger feelings of judgement, criticism, inadequacy and guilt. In this scenario you can try initiating the request for help by saying that you have researched the pros and cons of all feeding methods and have decided what is right for you and your baby, and would like help with the combination feeding, please. If this is ignored, you could perhaps say 'thank you for the information, but I have already made my decision', and repeat the request for help with combination feeding.

The likelihood is that if you are asking for help, you may be in a vulnerable state of mind when any confrontation seems too stressful, so it can be very helpful to have a partner, family member or friend who will back you up. If that is not possible, then you have to learn to pretend to listen, then, when they have finished, smile politely and go and ask someone more helpful.

If you do not receive the help you feel you need, you are completely within your rights to ask them to leave and to speak to someone else.

CRITICS The same advice applies to anyone else who challenges your parenting decisions, no matter who they are or how impressive their CV or qualifications. Remember that behind all that they are just people, like you and me, and as such are likely to have their own preconceptions and biases as any other opinionated person in the street.

They do not know you or your baby or your lifestyle; they just know their own specialist subject, so if you feel criticised, judged or ignored, then either reiterate that you are happy with your parenting choices and only need help with this particular problem, try to ignore it and focus on the problem at hand or leave and seek help elsewhere. If there is no one else to speak to, then hold onto the knowledge that you are a caring, intelligent adult quite capable of making the right choices for your child, and try not to let their opinions upset you or undermine your confidence.

Any healthcare professional or specialist you approach should, at the very least, be courteous and supportive, and if they are not, then it is reasonable to complain about them to their professional body. You do not deserve poor treatment.

Hospital

When you are in hospital, you can ask the nurses and midwives for help regarding anything at all to do with your baby, for example breastfeeding, bottle-feeding (expect a lecture!), handling baby, nappy-changing, cord, winding, and so on, so any questions you have, no matter how basic, just ask. Some hospitals provide access to lactation consultants, and will also refer you to any other specialist help you might require.

Community midwife

Once home, in the UK you are under the care of a community midwife for the next two weeks, so again, any problems, questions or doubts you have you can refer to them.

Health visitor

After two weeks (UK) you will be signed off by the midwife and your information handed over to the health visitor. They usually work in teams, and are linked with one or more doctors' surgeries in your catchment area.

Health visitors are nurses or midwives who have undergone further training, and are responsible for your child's welfare until they reach school age. They can offer advice on vaccinations, feeding, development, weaning, sleep, routines, and so on, and they will have good knowledge of local support groups, baby and toddler groups and medical facilities. They can also help with anxiety, stress and postnatal depression, and can refer you or your baby to various experts and give you advice on how to go about getting the help you need.

Health visitors can be either completely wonderful or absolutely terrible, and what sort you get is the luck of the draw. I have met ones who are so lovely, well informed and supportive that I could hug them, and others who are grumpy, belligerent and ignorant (often in densely populated areas where they are seriously overworked) and have made me want to bash my head against a wall.

The most common complaint used to be that they would push formula at the expense of breastfeeding, but this has now switched to the polar opposite, and any mention of formula or bottles is likely to be met with frowns and lectures. This is partly due to policy decisions over which they have no control, but how they interpret and implement those decisions reflects very much their own personal beliefs and biases, so some will support your decisions and give you the help you need, while others can give you a hard time.

If you get one of the latter kind, just call the health team, state that you do not wish to see that particular health visitor, explain why and ask for a different one next time. Not surprisingly, they are used to this sort of request and deal with it accordingly.

If you do have a serious problem with a particular health visitor, it is important to remember that allowing them access to your home is *not compulsory*. They have no rights and you do not have to see them, not even to have your baby weighed. They are strictly a service for your benefit, not a legal requirement, though the majority of the time they are very useful and helpful.

They usually visit once or twice, and if everything looks to be going well, they come only if you request a visit due to a problem you are encountering, and you can call on them any time you are worried about something. They usually hold weekly drop-in clinics at a doctor's surgery or medical centre, which can be useful if you want to have baby weighed or have any questions.

Doctor/GP

If a midwife or health visitor believes that you or your baby needs non-urgent medical attention, they will suggest you get an appointment with your doctor, and often this is the first step for any concerned parent.

The problem can sometimes be knowing when 'probably nothing' becomes 'maybe something' and you wonder if it should be checked out by a doctor.

There is a lot of reliable information on sensible, well-informed websites such as NHS Choices, and most baby books have basic information that can guide you such as I have covered in Chapter 9, but beyond that you must trust your instinct. If something is worrying you then you must get it checked out. I know that some parents feel they may be seen as 'over fussy' by some doctors, but if that is their attitude, then that is their problem, not yours. They are paid to examine patients for signs of ill health either physical, mental or emotional, so do not hesitate to seek their opinion when you have a concern.

Most doctors I have encountered have been very helpful and supportive of new parents, with only a few being dismissive or offhand, so please don't worry about it.

Apart from diagnosing and prescribing, your GP is often the first step in the process of getting further help, as they can refer you on to consultants and specialists and have knowledge of what help is available in your area. If you are using the NHS, there are usually waiting times of weeks or sometimes months for a consultant's appointment, so the earlier you contact your doctor the better.

Your GP will also be able to help you with issues such as anxiety and depression, and surgeries often have lists of local support groups, so please do not hesitate to make use of them to keep yourself well.

Non-medical expert, 'consultant'

More and more nowadays we are seeing and hearing about experts who specialise in particular problems, with sleep consultants and lactation or breastfeeding consultants being the most common, but who also include babywearing consultants, weaning experts, potty-trainers and pretty much everything else baby related.

There are also maternity nurses who will come and work on a twenty-four-hour basis for five or six days in your home, or for weeks or even months depending on your needs and budget, and there are further options for daily help or night nurses.

There are a lot of maternity nurses such as myself who also offer their experience, with face-to-face meetings or Skype and phone consultations followed by phone and email support. This can be an invaluable and affordable way of getting expert help when you most need it, and sometimes a half-hour phone chat with one of these people can turn your problem around without ever needing to meet face to face.

But beware!

There is currently *no regulation* of nannies, maternity nurses and non-medical childcare experts or consultants of any kind in the UK, so absolutely *anyone* can set themselves up as an expert yet have no training or experience at all.

The exception are childminders, who are very tightly regulated.

All someone has to do is build themselves a website, create a fictional CV with fake references, advertise in the right places and they are in business – mainly because, unbelievably, very few people actually check references.

YOU MUST CHECK REFERENCES Without regulation and professional bodies, the *only* way to find out if someone is who and what they claim to be is to check their references, and not just the last one, because that is too easy to rig using a friend or relative. You *must* check at least three references, and choose from those over the last two years, preferably spaced out over time, not the most recent three, and speak to the former client in person, not by email.

Do not be fooled by price. The most expensive consultants are not always the best, especially as people who are out to deceive you know full well that people assume expensive means good.

During a recent conversation with reputable fellow maternity nurses, it soon became appallingly obvious that very few clients bothered to check even one reference before hiring a complete stranger to care for their precious baby, putting both baby and themselves at risk from poor care and bad advice that could cause serious distress, if not worse.

I know that when you are stressed and exhausted it is very easy to be taken in by well-crafted, reassuring and impressive websites and CVs, but you *must* check, to safeguard yourself and your baby.

A good maternity nurse, nanny or consultant/expert will have lots of good references going back years (expect at least five years' experience from anyone claiming to be a consultant), and will have a current Paediatric First Aid Certificate (not a general First Aid Certificate) and a DBS (Disclosure and Barring Service) security check.

CHECK AND DOUBLE-CHECK If they have worked through an agency, call the agency and ask for a verbal reference. You can also try checking on local baby and child Facebook groups to see if anyone else has employed them before, or ask at mother and toddler groups.

I and fellow maternity nurses know of several people advertising in the childcare sector whose CVs we know to be blatant lies, claiming to have worked for celebrities and cared for impossible numbers of babies for the amount of time they have been in childcare.

Beware also of claims of X number of years in 'childcare', because that may just mean they have had two children and done some babysitting or childminding. (You could try googling them to check their experience.) If you want help with a baby aged under six months, make sure that their experience is with this age group. A former nanny may have ten years' experience, but only six months of that was with newborns. A health visitor may have ten years' experience within her field, but no experience at all of a live-in position or troubleshooting role, and they are *very* different.

Read between the lines, question what you are reading – investigate thoroughly.

Maternity nurse or nanny agency

As a stressed and exhausted parent, if all this is too much for you to face, there is always the option of finding help through an agency. A reputable agency will have checked references and insisted on up-to-date Paediatric First Aid and DBS Certificates, and will also have personal knowledge of the candidate you are considering.

There are plenty of agencies who provide maternity nurses and nannies, and an increasing number who provide day and night nurses, plus a few offering sleep and feeding consultants.

Beyond the checks, some agencies do little more than advertise your job and send you the details of those who apply, but this in itself will give you peace of mind about who you engage.

The very best agencies do much more than that. For instance, the maternity section of the agency that I get a lot of my work through, Eden Private Staff (edenprivatestaff.com), I hold up as an example of excellence because they have taken the time to get to know me and my strengths, my working style and my areas of expertise. At the same time, they also get to know potential clients and pride themselves on making a good match, one based not just on the baby care itself, but on personality and parenting styles and any other needs that may affect the placement.

This way, I know I will only interview with clients whose needs match my skills, and the parents know they will not be sent any unsuitable candidates. There are other agencies with similar standards, so call them and find out how they will process your request and what you can expect by way of applicants.

You will have to pay an agency fee, so be sure to check how much this is so you don't get a surprise when they invoice you, but within that fee you get the reassurance that candidates and their CVs have been thoroughly checked, that the agency will find you a replacement maternity nurse if for some reason she cannot complete the booking or if you don't get on, and they will help you with any questions you have regarding the booking.

Support group

There are support groups for pretty much every aspect of baby and childcare you can think of, so whatever problem you are facing, somewhere there will be support for you.

These groups can be physical, often run by charities, where you can go along and join a group or get advice in person. Others may offer support via the telephone using hotline numbers, and yet others are online via social media sites.

There are both advantages and disadvantages to all these types of groups.

FACE TO FACE With a physical group you can get a tremendous sense of support and camaraderie, but there may not be one local enough to you, or there may be waiting lists or appointment systems which, if you want immediate support, may be frustrating. You may also not feel emotionally up to dealing with whatever the problem is face to face, especially with strangers, or the transport difficulties may put you off.

TELEPHONE Hotline numbers can be immediate, and provide help and support accessed without even having to leave your house, but some people find them impersonal, so just think about your own preferred way of communicating and how you feel emotionally or physically when considering reaching out for help.

ONLINE GROUPS There are numerous groups on Facebook, many of which have been set up by parents who have faced, or are facing, the same problems you may be experiencing, for example reflux, colic, illness, abnormalities, postnatal depression, and so on. There are also groups that focus on specific parenting styles and choices which can offer support, friendship, advice and ideas, so it is worth exploring to see what's out there.

But a word of warning.

As I am sure you know by now, there is a lot of judgement, misinformation, criticism, pressure and even bullying being experienced within the parenting world at the moment, and a great deal of this takes place on, and is fuelled by, social media.

Please be careful about what you expose yourself to online, as the resulting damage to your confidence and emotional state can be severe.

Quite often you will hear about groups from friends, so before joining, take a moment to ask a few questions about members' attitudes in the group. Are they welcoming and supportive to everyone, or just to those who agree with the loudest members of the group? For instance, it may be a local group for a particular area, but if the dominant members are very pro-breastfeeding and you are bottle- or combination-feeding, you may find your-self being judged and criticised. If you are doing babywearing or attachment parenting, are there others in the group with the same parenting attitudes, or are they going to insult or make fun of you? Is the group well moderated and bullies blocked, or is it a free-for-all?

While it may be amusing to watch arguments when it involves someone else and you are feeling OK, it is not so funny when it centres around you and you are feeling vulnerable and insecure, so think carefully about your own personality and situation and take sensible measures to protect yourself.

There are some really excellent groups out there, so if you feel you need online interaction then invest some time and effort in seeking out the good groups, because I know from personal experience the level of companionship and support that such groups can inspire.

My absolute favourite online resource for information and support for anything at all to do with feeding is a group called The Fed is Best Foundation (fedisbest.org). This US-based group is totally dedicated to providing parents with the information and support they need in order to feed their baby to the best of their ability, and in the way that suits them best.

They are also campaigning for equality in education and sup-port for safe breastfeeding, formula-feeding, combination-feeding and tube-feeding.

They are uniquely non-judgemental and non-biased, and their information and advice is based on the latest, most up-to-date science, not on the hearsay, rumour and lies that currently plague the parenting community.

I am an official advocate of their mission, and together we are working to set up a sister group, The Fed is Best UK, in order to improve the situation in Britain.

If you do begin to suspect that online pressure may be affecting you negatively, then my advice would be to stay away. Stop getting notifications from the groups that bother you and block any abusive or unfriendly individuals, and, if necessary, take a break from all social media until you feel confident and strong enough to revisit them.

I hope this has given you some idea of what help is available to you, or has at least given you some ideas about who to ask or where to start looking.

I am also compiling an exhaustive list of sources of help on my website, and will only include those either tried and tested by myself, or that come highly recommended by friends and colleagues, so you know you will be in good hands.

11.

Emergency action

SCREAMING BABY –
HOW TO SHUT DOWN A MELTDOWN

This is advice and suggestions for you to use in emergency situations when baby is screaming and you are exhausted and desperate.

We are not thinking 'politically correct' or 'long term' or even 'chosen parenting styles' . . . we are just thinking about surviving!

The Baby Detective **AIM** process will help you to solve problems, but in order to work through it you first need to be able to think straight, which you can't begin to do if baby is screaming.

The aim here is simply to calm and quieten your screaming baby in order to give you time and space to think.

Comfort sucking

Offer baby a pacifier or a clean finger (little finger, short nail, upside down so nail lies on the tongue and soft pad towards the roof of the mouth).

Too wound up to take it? Wiggle it around or stroke the roof of the mouth. Still not taking it? Add a flavour, whatever is to hand. Just a **tiny drop** can surprise them enough to stop scream-ing. Suggestions – Infacol, gripe water, herbal tea, fruit juice, sugar water. Still not working? Move on to motion.

Movement

Hold baby upright against your chest *facing inwards* and walk around, dance around gently or bouncily, sway, bounce on the edge of the bed or on a yoga ball, do squats or pliés, heel raises, or a bouncy walk. Try the rocking chair. Try the stairs.

Turn baby to *face outwards* and repeat all the previous suggestions.

SWADDLE Swaddle baby really tightly and try everything again or, if baby was already swaddled, then try the opposite and un-swaddle them

Nothing working? Then you need to up the stakes to get their attention. Hold baby securely under both armpits, facing you, raise them up towards the ceiling until your arms are fully ex-tended, then bring them down again smoothly, but not too slowly. Remember, you are trying to surprise them, not soothe them. Try this gently and, if it doesn't work, try doing it again more quickly (just be aware of wobbly heads) and repeat a few times.

Remember we are trying to catch baby's attention long enough for them to start thinking about calming down, so big movements are unusual enough to be very effective. You are not trying, how-ever, to frighten them and must always take good care of their head and neck.

You can do the same thing by putting them in the car seat and swinging it. This is hard on your back, so I protect myself by resting one hand against the wall as a support.

Have the pacifier handy so that any time you see baby calming down, you can offer it again.

Noise

Noise makes an excellent distraction. Try making a 'Sssssh!' noise as loud as you possibly can (or use a sound app) to get their attention.

Try playing music or singing. If quiet and calm doesn't work, try loud and lively.

Light

If you are doing this in the dark and it doesn't work then try making the room brighter, turn on the television or stand in front of a window. Anything to distract them from crying.

Try a different room

Kitchens and bathrooms work wonderfully because they have spotlights and shiny appliances, and you can turn on taps for white noise. You can also hold their hands or feet under warm running water and talk or sing to them in front of mirrors.

If you have been in a light room, try going in to a dimly lit one or a pitch black one (just don't fall over anything!).

Air movement

You can gently blow on their faces, or stand in front of an open window or a fan. This often helps because crying babies get very hot and bothered, so a fan can be refreshing as well as distracting.

Other things to try

Try bathing baby, or taking baby in the bath or shower with you. It may relax you both.

Try putting baby in the sling/baby carrier around the house, or out on a walk. Even if they are very small you can still face them outwards, allowing them to be distracted. Just make sure you *support their head* at all times.

A trip in the car or pram/buggy might help.

Hand them over to another person, or ask other children to distract them.

Any time you sense that the crying is getting a bit quieter, or there are breaks or pauses between screams (not just for catching breath), then *try the pacifier or finger again* and see if you can get them to accept it (remember to wiggle it or add a flavour).

Once you have them sucking you can start trying to calm everything down by holding them closer to you, turning down music/noise/lights etc.

You will both be exhausted, so the aim is to get to the point where you can sit and cuddle baby somewhere comfortable, and to relax. Once you get to this stage make sure you give yourselves plenty of time to recover. Don't give it five minutes then try and put baby down to sleep, or start checking your phone etc. Wait until you are sure baby is calm and settled before you start doing anything else that might disturb them.

If you think baby is hungry then *this* is the point when you can offer milk.

This is the most extreme example of the importance of the trial and error process you are ever likely to experience as a parent so embrace it with confidence and imagination.

Try my suggestions but also use them as the jumping off point for your own ideas. Get creative (desperation is a great motivator!) and never be downhearted if something doesn't work, just try something else and eventually *you* will find what works for *your* baby in that particular situation, even if you have to try a hundred different things.

Just remember that all parents will go through something similar at some point on their parenting adventure, so you are not alone!

Emergency Routine

The whole premise of this book is to stress that one-size-fits-all approaches and routines are *not* the answer, and that you have to find what works for you and for your baby, so I refrained from including any generalised routines.

However, whilst helping a client recently during a Skype consultation I realised that I *do* have a failsafe routine that I recommend when parents are experiencing difficulties and need some sort of stability in a hurry and that is what I am going to share with you here.

7.00am   Feed
10.00am   Feed
1.00pm   Feed
4.00pm   Feed
7.00pm   Feed
10.00pm   Feed
Plus whatever night feeds you do.

I have started the day at 7am because that is manageable for most people, but whether you start at 6am or 8am just feed fairly strictly at three hourly intervals (always time from the beginning of the feed for better accuracy and consistency).

Swaddle your baby firmly for all daytime and night-time sleeps. A tired, stressed and screaming baby will really appreciate the security that a swaddle gives them, and it makes it much easier for them to cope with being put down to sleep, and then to stay asleep. If you have never swaddled your baby, it is fine to start anytime up to about eight weeks. I have successfully started later than that, but not later than three months. Once you have started, you can keep swaddling for as long as you can physically keep baby wrapped, but most babies don't need it after four or five months.

Always wake your baby for the feed no matter how much you hate doing it – you are trying to establish a routine which your baby's body will adapt to, so you must be consistent or there is no point in doing it. The fact that your baby will be having shorter sleeps in the day means that they are much more likely to sleep longer at night and will go a long way to help turn around the 'nocturnal baby' that sleeps all day and wakes all night.

Even if they are very tired, keep waking them as much as you can over the feeding hour e.g. feed, wind, feed, wind, nappy change, feed, wind, face wash, feed, wind. This will ensure that they have a full tummy and no wind so they will be settled until the next feed three hours later.

Always try to get your baby to bring up as much wind up as possible. Keep winding, there is always more there than you think. Every time you pick baby up, or change position (yours or theirs) becomes another opportunity to wind. Check out Chapter 6 for ideas and positions, and keep on winding even if baby is asleep by using the more passive techniques.

Don't worry about losing milk supply if you are breastfeeding. Six feeds a day plus another one or two in the night is sufficient stimulation to maintain your milk supply and may even improve it, because you will be less stressed and more able to rest, which has a massive impact on milk supply.

Don't let baby snack between feeds. Use a pacifier, or any other method you can think of to keep to the feeding schedule. It will only take twenty-four hours to break a snacking habit as long as you follow the advice above and make sure they feed really well.

Remember: in this situation I am not suggesting a permanent routine (though if you find it suits you and your baby, then by all means carry it on).

This is a routine for those times when:

- Your baby is screaming
- You feel like crying
- You are getting no sleep
- You feel like everything is falling apart
- You can't cope anymore
- You don't know what to do or who to turn to for help
- You can't wait another minute for help

This is a tried and tested routine that I have found babies respond to very quickly because it meets all their needs. If you follow it *consistently* for three days it will provide you and your baby with an element of stability and predictability, and allow everyone to calm down and begin to relax.

It will hopefully give you the breathing space you so desperately need, a starting point from which you can then go on and work through my **AIM** process, to find out what was causing problems in the first place, and to work towards your own ideal routine.

12.

Summary

Imagine that you want a career change and decide to set up your own business working from home. It is a new venture, out of your comfort zone, but you are confident that you can make it work.

On the first day your partner helps, which is great, but the next day your family starts dropping by and offering suggestions and well-meaning advice.

On the third day your friends start arriving, trying to be helpful, closely followed on the fourth day by acquaintances, work colleagues, and then even random strangers from the street – all offering advice, making suggestions, criticising, second guessing your decisions and judging. They never go home, never stop, even through the night. Everywhere you turn there is someone 'trying to help'

By the end of two weeks you are exhausted, stressed and confused, your confidence is in tatters, you don't trust your own judgement and you have forgotten that you ever thought you could manage your new business.

This is what parenting today has become – a never ending stream of information and opinion that confuses and erodes confidence.

By writing this book and by sharing my process of Assessment, Investigation and Modification, I believe I can help to lead you back to a place of confidence. From there, I firmly believe that you will become adept at sifting through the information and advice that threatens to drown new and prospective parents, decide what is relevant and useful to you, your baby and your situation, and discard the rest. I want you to become so confident that you are able to silence and ignore all the voices that confuse and criticise, and to have faith in your own ability to make the best choices for you and your family.

I sincerely hope that my book helps you become the ultimate Baby Detective, easily capable of solving any problem, meeting any challenge, adapting to any situation, and most importantly of al, being able to relax and enjoy your life as a parent.

I will continue working towards this aim through my babycare blog at www.babydetective.co.uk so please come and join me there for positive, helpful, accurate and unbiased information.

Good luck and have faith in yourself . . . you can do this!

Sarah x

Acknowledgements

This book was written out of a determination to try and help as many parents and babies as possible by sharing my knowledge and experience, and it is hard to believe that it is finally finished and out there in the world . . . my literary newborn!

I am truly grateful for this chance to thank those precious people who have inspired, supported and believed in me over the last three years.

Firstly I want to thank Sienna for opening my eyes to a world of possibilities and to how wonderful life can be when you dedicate yourself completely to something you love.

To Jenny Brown . . . your random act of kindness led me to my agents and I will never forget that you took a moment to help someone you had never met.

To my agents Graham Maw Christie, thank you for taking me on and being tirelessly patient and efficient, especially Jane who acted as interpreter between the world I knew and the world I was entering.

Thank you to Amanda Harris, my publisher at Orion, for having such strong faith in me and believing in my book from the very beginning.

Special thanks to Olivia Morris, my editor, who understood what I was trying to say and helped craft my words into this wonderful book with skill and humour.

To Natali Drake, fellow first time author. Thank you for sharing this journey with me. There have been times when only you understood what I was going through and you have helped more than you know.

To my brother James and his wife Kerry, I can't tell you what it has meant to me over the last year to have your friendship, your humour, your spare room . . . and Kerry's gin ! You have supported, encouraged and distracted me through the strangest year of my life (so far!).

To all the ladies who hide in the Loo . . . you know who you are. I truly feel that I have a virtual home with you and the strength, courage and love that I see every day is humbling and inspiring. Thank you Emma Gibbard for creating this group.

In my working life I have come across a few families that hold a special place in my heart and who have all encouraged my book dream so a special thank you to Diana and James, Rebecca and Heron, Michelle and Super Zeke, Constance and Jonty, Jaime and Jonny.

Finally, and most importantly, my heartfelt thanks to every single parent and baby I have had the pleasure and honour to have worked with over the years. You have taught me so much and have been the inspiration for this book.

You have given meaning to my life.

Index